PURCHASE THE COMPLETE BOOK
Bible Law vs.
the United States Constitution
AT A DISCOUNT RATE

This primer is the shortened version of the book by the same name. If you would like to read the complete book, you can use this coupon to purchase it with the price of the primer discounted.

ORDER THE COMPLETE VERSION OF
Bible Law vs. the United States Constitution
FOR ONLY $12 ($7 OFF).

The complete version contains almost 700 pages of documented quotes, point-by-point comparisons of the Bible and the Constitution, and in-depth discussions on the modern application of Biblical laws.

Fill out the form below and include **$12 + $4 S&H**. We accept cash, checks, or money orders (make out to Mission to Israel Ministries).
   Mail to: Mission to Israel, PO Box 248, Scottsbluff, NE 69363.

- -

Name: _____

Address: _____

City: _____ State: _____ Zip: _____

Phone # (optional): _____

Email (optional): _____

D1250407

BIBLE LAW
VS.
THE UNITED STATES CONSTITUTION

The Christian Perspective

(A Primer)

BIBLE LAW
VS.
THE UNITED STATES
CONSTITUTION

The Christian Perspective

(A Primer)

TED R. WEILAND

MISSION TO ISRAEL
Scottsbluff, Nebraska

Published by Mission to Israel Ministries
PO Box 248
Scottsbluff, Nebraska 69363
www.missiontoisrael.org

Printed in the United States of America

ISBN 978-0-9755943-9-1

Also by Ted R. Weiland:

God's Covenant People: Yesterday, Today and Forever

Christian Duty Under Corrupt Government: A Revolutionary Commentary on Romans 13:1-7

The Phinehas Hoods: A Biblical Examination of Unscriptural Vigilantism

Capital Punishment: Deterrent or Catalyst?

Prisons: Shut Them All Down!

Marriage, Divorce, & Remarriage

Eve: Did She or Didn't She? The Seedline Hypothesis Under Scrutiny

Israel's Identity: It Matters!

Spiritual Israel: Out of All Nations or Out of the Nation of Israel?

The Mystery of the Gentiles: Who Are They and Where Are They Now?

Baptism: All You Wanted to Know and More

The Ten Commandments Series:
Thou shalt have no other gods before me
Thou shalt not make unto thee any graven image
Thou shalt not take the name of YHWH thy God in vain
Remember the sabbath day, to keep it holy
Honour thy father and thy mother
Thou shalt not kill
Thou shalt not commit adultery
Thou shalt not steal
Thou shalt not bear false witness
Thou shalt not covet

TABLE OF CONTENTS

With this primer, I hope to motivate you to think about the United States Constitution, a document few Americans have read and to which fewer yet have given any serious thought, especially from a Biblical paradigm. More importantly, I hope to inspire you to study Yahweh's* law and to esteem it as did the Psalmist, who declared his love for the law seven times in Psalm 119.** I also hope to create a vision for Yahweh's kingdom *here on earth* as it is in heaven (Matthew 6:10).***

This primer is the shortened version of the book by the same name. If you come across something that piques your interest, it is probably dealt with in much more detail in the complete book, which you can purchase on our website at missiontoisrael.org/books-summary.php.

---

*YHWH (most often pronounced Yahweh) is the English transliteration of the Tetragrammaton, the principal Hebrew name of the God of the Bible.[1]

**See Chapter 1 "The Perfect Law of Yahweh," in the full version of *Bible Law vs. the United States Constitution* (missiontoisrael.org/biblelaw-constitutionalism-pt1.php), for scriptural evidence that Yahweh's moral laws are still applicable under the New Covenant.

***See Chapter 2 "The Kingdom: Yesterday, Today, and Forever," in the full version of *Bible Law vs. the United States Constitution* (missiontoisrael.org/biblelaw-constitutionalism-pt2.php), for scriptural evidence that Yahweh's kingdom is extant here on earth now.

OUR NATIONAL IDOL

Christians* have a responsibility to uphold Christian principles in every aspect of life – including government. Christians looking to create a better government will not achieve a nation that pleases Yahweh by promoting the Constitution. Why? The Constitution is not the Christian document we have been told it is, but actually conflicts with Christianity and, in many locations, is hostile to Yahweh's morality.

How can I say this, especially when so many sources appear to authenticate the Constitution as a Christian document, created by Christian men? The Constitution is largely touted as a Christian document. But is it? Have you ever studied its contents and compared it to that of the Scriptures? I have, and I was astounded by what I found. How can a document that promotes the will *of* the people over Yahweh's will *for* his people, be the answer to America's current national crisis?

Although Christians expose and combat sin on many fronts, very few identify the Constitution as an idol of national prominence.

> It is possible for an idol to become so entrenched in the fabric of society that even the people of God fail to recognize it for what it is and to take steps to get rid of it. Our modern idols are not always easy to detect. They often take the shape of ideas and institutions woven into the warp and woof of our culture.[3]

The Constitution embodies the following Biblical infractions, among others:

---

*Not everyone claiming to be a Christian has been properly instructed in the Biblical plan of salvation. Mark 16:15-16; Acts 2:36-41, 22:1-16; Romans 6:3-4; Galatians 3:26-27; Colossians 2:11-13; and 1 Peter 3:21 should be studied to understand what is required to be covered by the blood of Jesus and forgiven of your sins.[2]

3

- The Preamble's substitution of a new national god for Yahweh.
- Article 1's usurpation of Yahweh's legislative powers.
- Article 2's commandeering of Yahweh's executive sovereignty.
- Article 3's supplanting of Yahweh's judgments.
- Article 6's repudiation of Christianity.
- Amendment 1's promotion of pluralism, polytheism, and idolatry.
- Amendment 2's replacement of the Biblical responsibility to bear arms.
- Amendment 8's condemnation of Yahweh's judgments.

THE PREAMBLE

WE THE PEOPLE of the United States, in order to form a more perfect union, establish justice, ensure domestic tranquility, provide for the common defence, promote the general welfare, and secure the blessings of liberty to ourselves and our posterity, do ordain and establish this Constitution for the United States of America.

Constitutionalists* often claim the Constitution was divinely inspired, and it *was* – by the new god known as WE THE PEOPLE. Yahweh was formally abandoned when the constitutional framers penned the first three words of the Preamble and put their signatures to the social compact. WE THE PEOPLE became the national replacement for Yahweh.

The United States Constitutional Republic is one of many governments in which the people have replaced Yahweh as the god of their society. There is no escaping theocracy. A government's laws reflect its morality, and the source of that morality (or, more often than, not immorality) is its god. It is never a question of theocracy or no theocracy, but *whose* theocracy. The people, by way of their elected officials, are the source of the Constitutional Republic's laws. Therefore, the Constitutional Republic's god is WE THE PEOPLE.

People recoil at the idea of a theocracy's morality being forced upon them, but because all governments are theocracies, someone's morality is always being enforced. This is an inevitability of government. The question is which god, theocracy, laws, and morality will we choose to live under?

---

*I am employing the term "Constitutionalists" in reference both to those who are formal members of the Constitution Party and to anyone else who believes in and endorses the Constitution.

All governments are theocentric – god-centered. This is true of a government of, by, and for Yahweh, and it is true of a government of, by, and for the people. Herein we find the battle so often described in the Bible: the war between Yahweh's will and man's will:

> It is better to trust in YHWH* than to put confidence in man. It is better to trust in YHWH than to put confidence in princes.
>
> Psalm 118:8-9**

The first three words of the Preamble are an expression of this eternal conflict.

Constitution vs. Constitution

> In June of 1639 the leading men of New Haven [Connecticut] held a convention in a barn, and formally adopted the Bible as the constitution of the State. Everything was strictly conformed to the religious standard. The government was called the House of Wisdom.... None but church members were admitted to the rights of citizenship.
>
> *History of the United States*, 1874[5]

The constitutional form of government established in the late 1700s was *not* practiced in the 1600s or early 1700s. A change of law and government occurred in the late 1700s, not only from English rule but also from the Colonies' Biblically based governments. From that moment on, the nation that had been predominately Christian became progressively secular and humanistic:

> A nation's religious foundation can be determined by looking at its economic system, judicial pronouncements, educational goals, and taxing policy. Culture is "religion externalized." Look at the nation's art and music, and there you will find its religion. Read its books and newspapers. Watch its television programs. The outgrowth of civilization will be present on every page and in every program.

---

*Where the Tetragrammaton (YHWH) – the four Hebrew characters that represent the personal name of God – has been unlawfully rendered the LORD or GOD in English translations, I have taken the liberty to correct this error by inserting YHWH where appropriate.[4]

**All Scripture is quoted from the King James Version, unless otherwise noted. Portions of Scripture have been omitted for brevity. If you have questions regarding any passage, please study the text to ensure it has been properly used.

The habits of individuals and families are also indicators of a nation's religious commitments. The sum of all these expressions will lead us to a nation's religious commitments. While it might be beneficial to look at the creeds of the churches, the actions of the people who subscribe to the creeds are a more accurate barometer of what the people really believe.[6]

The change of law and government in the late 1700s brought about a change of religion, and because the former law and government represented Yahweh, both He and His laws were necessarily discarded for the new god and its laws.

This is difficult to accept, especially since we have been told the framers were such godly men. Today's Christian Constitutionalists are quick to share the framers' Christian-sounding quotations. Hundreds of books, replete with such quotations, have been compiled, and no one can question that many of the framers and their disciples often said the right things regarding Yahweh, His Son, Christianity, and occasionally even His laws. But such statements mean nothing by themselves. Thomas Jefferson made Christian-sounding statements, but no one would argue that Jefferson was a Christian.

Some people seem to believe the only thing necessary to prove one's godliness or Christianity is an invocation of God. This erroneous and dangerous assumption opens the door to political abuse in the name of Christ and the Christian sanction of ungodly actions – including those of the constitutional framers.

Recognizing the Bible and Christianity's influence upon society is not the same as legislating and adjudicating according to Yahweh's laws. One only needs to look at the record to know there has been a dearth of the latter since the Constitution's ratification. In order to conclude the framers were Christians, today's Christian Constitutionalists have severed the framers' words from their actions. To date, the battle between Christians and secularists over the Constitution has been a war of quotations – and there are plenty to go around for both sides, *often from the same framers*. The only means of determining whether the framers were Christians is to compare their actions to the Word of God:

> Not every one that saith unto me, Lord, Lord, shall enter into the kingdom of heaven; but he that doeth the will of my Father which

7

is in heaven. Many will say to me in that day, Lord, Lord, have we not prophesied in thy name? And in thy name have cast out devils? And in thy name done many wonderful works? And then will I profess unto them, I never knew you: depart from me, ye that work iniquity (*anomian* – lawlessness).

Matthew 7:21-23

This is a perfect description of the framers. Although some of them privately and publicly claimed to be Christians, they openly practiced anomianism. The framers nowhere attributed the inspiration for any specific article or amendment in the Constitution to the Bible or the laws of Yahweh. Worse, they created "laws" contrary to Yahweh's.

Internal Evidence

Humanism is the placing of Man at the center of all things and making him the measure all things.

Francis Schaeffer[7]

The Preamble is arguably the most brazen human claim to sovereignty ever written. If you stop and think about its presumptuous claims, you will see that this new constitution is humanism of the rankest sort:

…[Yahweh's] law is slacked [ignored, NASB], and judgment doth never go forth: for the wicked doth compass about the righteous; therefore wrong judgment proceedeth.

Habakkuk 1:4

The framers not only compromised Yahweh's law, they completely ignored it, and, in many instances, legislated against it. Constitutionalism is a collective, agreed-upon form of humanism. By their silence, and thus their acquiescence to this new form of government, the people claimed their authority, not from Yahweh, but from themselves.

Establishing Justice

They are terrible and dreadful: their judgment [justice, NASB] and their dignity shall proceed of themselves. …imputing this his power unto his god.

Habakkuk 1:7, 11

Not only did the Chaldeans' authority originate with themselves, but so did their justice. And so does the justice of WE THE PEOPLE: "WE THE PEOPLE of the United States, in order to form a more perfect union, establish justice…." What an audacious assertion. Only Yahweh is just, and only He can establish justice:

8

Justice and judgment are the habitation of thy [Yahweh's] throne:
mercy and truth shall go before thy face.
                                                    Psalm 18:14

Instead of confirming the justice inherent in Yahweh's morality and
already established in His perfect law, the framers' declaration implies
that justice had yet to be established. This (and other numerous confirm-
ations throughout the Constitution) reveals they preferred their own justice
to the justice of Yahweh. Otherwise, they would have followed the
example of our Christian forefathers in the 1600s and early 1700s and
cited, or at least mentioned, the laws of Yahweh upon which their justice
was based.

A More Perfect Union

In contrast with New Haven's 1639 Agreement ("we all agree that
the scriptures hold forth a perfect rule for the direction of government"[8]),
one of the purposes for this new Constitution was "to form a more perfect
union." What the framers had in mind was a union "more perfect" than
that of the Articles of Confederation. However, because the Articles of
Confederation and the Constitution were both based upon the imperfect
laws of man, both were a far cry from the governments of the New Eng-
land Colonies. The framers were willing to settle for something *more*
perfect, which amounted to something far *less* than perfect.

Securing Liberty

As stated in the Preamble, another purpose of the Constitution is to
"secure the blessings of liberty to ourselves and our posterity." From
childhood, Americans are indoctrinated to believe that, thanks to the
Constitution, America is the freest nation on earth:

> The media … has played a key role in persuading people that we
> are the most free nation on earth. While this may or may not be
> true, most people have never considered this possibility: If all of
> the other nations were under 100% totalitarian dictatorships, and
> the United States of America was only under a 95% totalitarian
> dictatorship, it could still be said that "America is the most free
> nation on earth." So it is a rather meaningless boast.[9]

Convinced the Constitution would fail to secure and protect liberty,
Patrick Henry voiced his concerns to the Virginia Ratifying convention in
1788:

> ...I say our privileges and rights are in danger. ...the new form of Government ...will ... effectually ... oppress and ruin the people.... In some parts of the plan before you, the great rights of freemen are endangered, in other parts, absolutely taken away.... There will be no checks, no real balances, in this Government: What can avail your specious imaginary balances, your rope-dancing, chain-rattling, ridiculous ideal checks and contrivances? ...And yet who knows the dangers that this new system may produce: they are out of the sight of the common people: They cannot foresee latent consequences.... I see great jeopardy in this new Government.[10]

In contrast to the federalists' failed predictions, this and nearly everything the anti-federalists forecast about the Constitution has come true.

Except for occasional interference from the British kings across the Atlantic, this nation experienced its greatest liberty in the 1600s and early 1700s. From the ratification of the Constitution until now, our liberty has been whittled away. At present, we would be hard-pressed to find a nation with *less* liberty than the United States of America. As Pastor Mather Byles purportedly put it before the American War for Independence: "Which is better – to be ruled by one tyrant three thousand miles away, or by three thousand tyrants not a mile away?"

It is extremely difficult to convince well-fed, content, and happy Americans they are not free. But contentment has nothing to do with freedom. A slave is a slave even if he's fat and happy. "None are more hopelessly enslaved than those who falsely believe they are free."[11]

2 Corinthians 3:17 states, "...where the Spirit of the Lord is there is liberty." The Spirit of the Lord cannot be found in the Constitution because Yahweh and His perfect laws of liberty were flagrantly disregarded. The Constitution provided us, not with liberty, but with bondage: dishonest and reprobate legislators, an ungodly court system, corruption, licenses, permits, and countless registrations, in addition to taxes on nearly everything:

> Ye shall know them by their fruits. Do men gather grapes of thorns, or figs of thistles? Even so every good tree bringeth forth good fruit; but a corrupt tree bringeth forth evil fruit. A good tree cannot bring forth evil fruit, neither can a corrupt tree bring forth good fruit.
> Matthew 7:16-18

What has been the fruit of the Constitution? We have only to look at the historical record of the last 200-plus years to know the Constitution shackled us with slavery. Man-made surrogates never have and never will provide mankind with liberty. Only Yahweh, by way of Jesus'* blood-atoning sacrifice and resurrection, can free us as individuals, and only His perfect laws of liberty can free us as a nation.

Christians are incessantly claiming 2 Chronicles 7:14: "If my people, which are called by name, shall humble themselves, and pray, and seek my face, and turn from their wicked ways; then will I hear from heaven, and will forgive their sin, and will heal their land." Tragically, the very people who claim this verse fail to heed it:

> He that turneth away his ear from hearing the [Yahweh's] law, even his prayer shall be abomination.
>
> Proverbs 28:9

Because our prayers for national deliverance are not being answered, we have obviously failed to fulfill the requirements found in this verse. The Constitution represents our national idolatry, and until we repent of our veneration of WE THE PEOPLE and all it represents, we cannot expect Yahweh to hear our prayers and heal our land. In fact, such a request is akin to Joshua's prayer regarding Israel's defeat at Ai. Following is Yahweh's response:

> And YHWH said unto Joshua, Get thee up; wherefore liest thou thus upon thy face? Israel hath sinned, and they have also transgressed my covenant which I commanded them … I [will not] be with you any more, except ye destroy the accursed from among you. Up, sanctify the people, and say, Sanctify yourselves against to morrow: for thus saith YHWH God of Israel, There is an accursed thing in the midst of thee, O Israel: thou canst not stand before thine enemies, until ye take away the accursed thing from among you.
>
> Joshua 7:10-13

Until Christian Americans recognize and destroy the accursed thing in our midst, we have no reason to believe Yahweh will fulfill 2 Chronicles 7:14.

---

*Yeshua is the English transliteration of our Savior's given Hebrew name, with which He introduced Himself to Paul in Acts 26:14-15. (Jesus is the English transliteration of the Greek Iesous, which is the Greek transliteration of the Hebrew Yeshua.) Because many people are unfamiliar or uncomfortable with Yeshua, I have chosen to use the more familiar Jesus in this book in order to remove what might otherwise be a stumbling block.[12]

ARTICLE 1

All legislative powers herein granted shall be vested in a congress of the United States, which shall consist of a Senate and House of Representatives....

"Legislators"

Noah Webster's 1828 American Dictionary of the English Language defines the word "legislator": "A lawgiver; one who makes laws...."[13] With this definition in mind, measure Article 1 by the following declarations:

> For YHWH is our judge, YHWH is our lawgiver, YHWH is our king....
>
> Isaiah 33:22

> There is one lawgiver....
>
> James 4:12

As the source of morality, Yahweh is the source of all true law. Because legislation enacts morality, morality and legislation are indivisible. Yahweh holds the monopoly on legislation and thus on the determination of what is good and what is evil. For any man or group of men to legislate a different code is tantamount to calling good evil and evil good (Isaiah 5:20).

Article 1 begins "All legislative powers herein granted...." Granted by whom? Not by the God Yahweh, but by the god WE THE PEOPLE. You will look in vain to find any reference (inside or outside the Constitution) in which the framers affirmed the government's legislative powers were granted by Yahweh. Neither did they ever affirm the laws of Yahweh:

> Cursed be he that confirmeth not all the words of this law to do them. And all the people shall say, Amen.
>
> Deuteronomy 27:26

13

If we believe all morality originates with Yahweh, then we must conclude any law contrary to His law represents lawlessness, unrighteousness, and immorality. Because Yahweh is the sole legislator, only His legislation is law. Any attempt to make law contrary or in addition to His perfect law is ultimately futile, as demonstrated by the fickle propensity of constitutional "legislators":

> Two people could have walked down any U. S. street in 1930 – one with a bottle of whiskey under his arm and one with a bar of gold in his pocket, and the one with the whiskey would have been a criminal whereas the one with the bar of gold would have been considered a good law abiding citizen. If the same thing happened in any U. S. city in 1970, the one with the whiskey would be the law abiding citizen and the one with the gold bar would be the criminal.[14]

More importantly, any attempt to legislate outside Biblical parameters is a seditious act against Yahweh. Article 1 mandates public slavery to a congress that has the power to make "laws," not only in addition to, but in contradiction to Yahweh's laws. Since the Constitutional Convention, Congress has consistently legislated contrary to Yahweh's morality. This incessant supplanting of Yahweh's laws will continue until Americans recognize and repent of their constitutional idolatry.

Constitutional legislation authorizes a two-thirds majority to make *anything* "law" – including infanticide and protection of sodomites. That the federal government does not have jurisdiction to legalize infanticide and sodomy is technically true. However, this does not change the fact that it *did* legalize these and other abominations. Libertarian attorney Lysander Spooner (1808-1887) wrote that the Constitution "has either authorized such a government as we have had, or has been powerless to prevent it."[15]

Because Yahweh's law is perfect (Psalm 19:7), endeavors to improve upon it, via human legislators, are attempts to dethrone the King and commandeer His throne. This is what happened in the Garden, at the Tower of Babel, and when the people chose Saul over Yahweh as their king. It is what has been attempted every time our forefathers rejected Yahweh's perfect laws and chose man's surrogate laws to replace them.

Yahweh has the monopoly on legislation. If Christians truly believed Isaiah 33:22, they would refuse to use the word "legislators" for yesterday's constitutional framers and today's senators and representatives. They certainly would not look to the non-Biblical decrees of these "legislators" as law.

> Know therefore this day, and consider it in thine heart, that YHWH he is God in heaven above, and upon the earth beneath: there is none else. Thou shalt keep therefore his statutes, and his commandments, which I command thee this day, that it may go well with thee, and with thy children after thee, and that thou mayest prolong thy days upon the earth, which YHWH thy God giveth thee, for ever.
>
> Deuteronomy 4:39-40

ARTICLE 2

The executive power shall be vested in a President of the United States of America. He shall hold his office during the term of four years, and, together with the Vice President, chosen for the same term, be elected....

If the United States Executive Branch were necessary, Yahweh would have provided for it in His laws. He did not provide for presidents and vice presidents because He, Himself, is the everlasting King:

> For YHWH is our judge, YHWH is our lawgiver, YHWH is our king....
>
> Isaiah 33:22

Because the framers did not acknowledge the United States Constitution's subordination to Yahweh and His sovereignty, Article 2 can only be understood as a rejection of Yahweh's executive authority and an attempt to usurp His executive power.

Presidents, vice presidents, and their tax-paid cabinets and staffs are superfluous. This will initially be difficult to accept for the average American who cannot fathom government without a human executive leader. However, no executive branch except for Yahweh's Kingship existed in America before 1788. The government functioned without a president and vice president. *McGuffey's Eclectic Reader*, America's most popular school book in the 1800s, testified to America's early form of theocratic government:

> Their [the Puritans'] form of government was as strictly theocratical insomuch that it would be difficult to say where there was any civil authority among them distinct from ecclesiastical juris-diction. Whenever a few of them settled a town, they immediately

17

gathered themselves into a church; and their elders were magistrates, and their code of laws was the Pentateuch.... God was their King; and they regarded him as truly and literally so....[16]

Term Limits

Article 2 provides four-year terms for presidents. Amendment 22 limits presidents to two terms. Most people would concede term limits are a good thing when evil men rule. But the question Christians should be asking is whether term limits are Biblical. Consider Solomon's wisdom:

> For the transgression of a land many are the princes thereof: but by a man of understanding and knowledge the state thereof shall be prolonged.
>
> Proverbs 28:2

Yahweh intends the term of a ruler who keeps His laws to be protracted:

> And it shall be, when he sitteth upon the throne of his kingdom, that he shall write him a copy of this law in a book ... that he turn not aside from the commandment, to the right hand, or to the left: to the end that he may prolong his days in his kingdom....
>
> Deuteronomy 17:18-20

The Constitution provides for the United States to be ruled by ruler after ruler, which is part of Yahweh's judgment against a sinful nation. Although term limits prevent corrupt officials from serving *any longer* than their terms allow, they provide for them to serve *as long as* their terms allow. Term limits are a Band-Aid on a self-inflicted wound. Provided a man remains Biblically qualified and mentally capable, he would not need to be removed.

Elections

> ...the community put the legislative power into such hands as **they** think fit....
>
> John Locke[17]

Article 2 provides for the election of presidents. Voting has for so long been promoted as one of the United States' foundational and inviolable rights that it is sacrosanct to most Americans. To question the legitimacy of elections is almost tantamount to sedition – even in the eyes of the average Christian. Many Christians contend that voting is a god-given right, and it *is* a right – under the god WE THE PEOPLE.

Because Americans are inundated with propaganda declaring it unpatriotic not to vote, the recommendation that Christians not participate in elections is often met with hostility. Are we more concerned about being un-American or being unbiblical?

In addition to the continual brainwashing about how fortunate we are to have free elections, one of the reasons most Christians believe so strongly about protecting their right to vote is few of them have ever challenged elections from a Biblical paradigm. Some people attempt to use Jethro's counsel to his son-in-law Moses, as the Biblical precedent for elections:

> Moreover thou shalt provide out of all the people able men, such as fear God, men of truth, hating covetousness; and place such over them, to be rulers of thousands, and rulers of hundreds, rulers of fifties, and rulers of tens. Exodus 18:21

What is described here was not a popular election; it was a nomination of qualified men for Moses to appoint. An election is not necessary to select Biblically qualified men. Men either are Biblically qualified or they are not. Popularity determines elections; Biblical qualifications determine appointments. To assume Jethro's instructions called for elections is just that – an assumption. Jethro's counsel called for the appointment of rulers who would be judges, not the election of those who would be presidents. Among other things, an appointed leader must:

➤ Be a man.*
➤ Be a Christian.**
➤ Fear Yahweh, not man.
➤ Be schooled in the laws of Yahweh.

---

*See Chapter 28 "Amendment 19: The Curse of Women's Suffrage" in the full version of *Bible Law vs. the United States Constitution* (missiontoisrael.org/biblelaw-constitutionalism-pt28.php), for more regarding Yahweh's patriarchal qualification.
**Not everyone claiming to be a Christian has been properly instructed in the Biblical plan of salvation. Mark 16:15-16; Acts 2:36-41, 22:1-16; Romans 6:3-4; Galatians 3:26-27; Colossians 2:11-13; and 1 Peter 3:21 should be studied to understand what is required to be covered by the blood of Jesus and forgiven of your sins.[18]

➤ Write out his own copy of Yahweh's laws.
➤ Read Yahweh's laws daily.
➤ Observe the laws of Yahweh in his own life.
➤ Be humble.
➤ Be honest.
➤ Be just.
➤ Be impartial in judgment.
➤ Be immune to bribery.
➤ Be neither greedy nor covetous.
➤ Be a terror to the wicked and a champion of the righteous.*

Unlike Yahweh's system, which provides for the appointment of the best of the best – the Constitution compels people to elect the lesser of two evils. It also necessitates political parties that are not only unbiblical but whose platforms are invariably ungodly. Political parties are the mechanism by which Christian constituents are offered up on the altar of WE THE PEOPLE.

After every election, regardless who's elected, Americans eventually have cause for regret. And yet, every four years, they march right back to the voting booths with eternal hope (or is it merely short-sightedness?) and do it all over again. Elections provide us with a lose-lose proposition. On the other hand, when we have two or more Biblically qualified candidates, we end up with a servant of God, regardless who's appointed.

Through Yahweh's means of appointment by lot, man does the selecting and Yahweh does the electing. The term "election" is actually a Biblical expression, referring to Yahweh's choice of leaders, as required in Deuteronomy 17:15. Man has hijacked the term and replaced Yahweh's means of election with his own, by which (we hope) the better man, rather than Yahweh's *best* man, is chosen.

Of greater consequence, voters become accomplices in the crimes of those they elect. Paul warned Timothy of this consequence even as it pertains to appointments:

> Do not lay hands upon anyone too hastily and thus share responsibility for the sins of others; keep yourself free from sin.
> 1 Timothy 5:22, NASB

---

*Exodus 18:19-21; Deuteronomy 1:13-17, 17:15-20; 2 Samuel 23:3; 2 Chronicles 19:5-8; Jeremiah 30:21; Romans 13:1-4; 1 Timothy 3:1-13; and Titus 1:5-9.

As subjects of the King of kings, our duty is *not* to elect a candidate from a political party (including, and perhaps especially, the Constitution Party). Our duty is to establish Yahweh's judicial system and appoint men who fear Him and who will enforce His law rather than constitutional law.

ARTICLE 3

The judicial power of the United States, shall be vested in one supreme court, and in such inferior courts as the Congress may, from time to time, ordain and establish. The judges, both of the supreme and inferior courts, shall hold their offices during good behavior....

Christian Constitutionalists generally believe the provision for a superior and inferior court system was also derived from Jethro's counsel to Moses in Exodus 18:19-22. This passage *does* provide Biblical precedent for a graduated judicial system, but that is where any similarity ends. The Bible stipulates, among other things, that judicial appointees must be men of truth who fear Yahweh and hate covetousness. The Constitution requires no Biblical qualifications whatsoever. Nowhere does the Constitution stipulate that judges must rule on behalf of Yahweh, rendering decisions based upon His commandments, statutes, and judgments as required in Exodus 18. That not even one framer contended for Yahweh, as did King Jehoshaphat, speaks volumes about the framers' disregard for Him and His judicial system:

> And [King Jehoshaphat] set judges in the land throughout all the fenced cities of Judah, city by city, and said to the judges, Take heed what ye do: for **ye judge not for man, but for YHWH,** who is with you in the judgment.... And he charged them, saying, **Thus shall ye do in the fear of YHWH,** faithfully, and with a perfect heart.
>
> 2 Chronicles 19:5-9

R.J. Rushdoony described justices who do not represent Yahweh as political hacks:

> If the judge does not represent God's Law order, he is ultimately a political hack and hatchet man whose job it is to keep the people in line, protect the establishment, and in the process to feather his own nest....[19]

> ...the judge was not to be an impartial referee but a partisan champion of the law of God, actively concerned with bringing God's justice to bear on every situation "by requiting the wicked, by recompensing his way upon his own head; and by justifying the righteous, by giving him according to his righteousness" (II Chron. 6:23).[20]

If the framers had truly borrowed from the Bible, they would have provided Biblical qualifications for judges. However, anticipating their prohibition against Christian test oaths in Article 6, they could not require judges to fear Yahweh in Article 3. Yahweh's law *requires* judges to fear Yahweh; the Constitution *bans* the same qualification.

Good Behavior

The only qualification provided in Article 3 is that judges are to be men and women of good behavior. Of what worth is such a condition if good behavior is nowhere defined? In Mark 10:18, Jesus declared, "No one is good except God alone." Good behavior can be defined and understood only from the parameters of Yahweh and His morality. Any standard that leaves "good behavior" to the determination of humans is humanism.

The Supreme Court

> There is hardly a political question in the United States which does not sooner or later turn into a judicial one.
>
> Alexis de Tocqueville[21]

The Supreme Court, composed of one chief justice and eight associate justices, with its power to not only judge the facts of any case but also to interpret, judge, and overrule any "law" passed by Congress (what Gary North described as "retroactive legitimacy to legislation"[22]), makes the Supreme Court the powerhouse or "big god" of this polytheistic system.

The power of the people of the United States of America and their representatives is subject to the Judicial Branch, and ultimately the Supreme Court, which is essentially immune from any kind of censure. The real power or sovereignty of the United States government resides in a Biblically unqualified and nearly always Biblically adverse five-to-four majority. The United States government is ultimately under the control and direction of five lawyers. And why not? It was predominately lawyers in 1787 (thirty-four of the fifty-five delegates were lawyers) who framed the Constitution and gave ultimate power into the hands of their own kind. Otto Scott described one of the consequences of the "lawyers of Philadelphia" as a spiritual coup:

> The church ... was thrown out into the street by the lawyers of Philadelphia, who decided not to have a Christian country.... [I]n effect, they took all the promises of religion, the pursuit of happiness, safety, security, all kinds of things, and they set up a lawyers' paradise, and the church was disenfranchised totally.[23]

This is nearly identical to Jesus' denunciation of lawyers:

> Woe unto you, lawyers! For ye have taken away the key of knowledge: ye entered not in yourselves, and them that were entering in ye hindered.
> Luke 11:52

The key of knowledge is the law of Yahweh, and lawyers, including and especially the Philadelphia thirty-four, have altered that law:

> My people are destroyed for lack of **knowledge**: because thou hast rejected knowledge, I will also reject thee ... seeing thou hast forgotten **the law of thy God**....
> Hosea 4:6

The Supreme Legislator

> In the United States, rights are proclaimed in the Constitution, but they are defined by the Supreme Court, which the Constitution has established to provide a reliable and definitive interpretation of the law.[24]

Although Article 6 declares the Constitution the supreme law of the land, whoever has the power to interpret that law is the supreme legislator. Chief Justice Warren Burger commented on the landmark case

Marbury v. Madison (5 U.S. 1 Cranch 137), which established judicial review under Article 3 of the Constitution:

> The cornerstone of our constitutional history and system remains the firm adherence of the Supreme Court to the Marbury principle of judicial review that "someone must decide" what the Constitution means.[25]

James Madison concurred:

> I acknowledge, in the ordinary course of government, that the exposition of the laws and Constitution devolves upon the Judiciary.[26]

Inherently Flawed

Constitutionalists believe the superiority of the United States Judicial System is demonstrated in that even Supreme Court decisions can be overturned and made right by either future Supreme Court justices or by constitutional amendment. But history has proven the opposite is more likely. Furthermore, the injustices that often occur in the interim between a bad decision and a better decision would seldom, if ever, occur in a Biblical court.

Nothing demonstrates this fundamental defect better than *Roe v. Wade*, which constitutionally provided for millions of infants to be murdered. While Christian Constitutionalists wait for the Constitutional Republic's system to (they *hope*) correct itself, millions more infants are being murdered. Under Yahweh's law, not one infant would have been murdered.

Even when wrong decisions are overturned, they can be overturned again by a later court. Judicial records expose this capricious tendency of the United States juridical system.

> ...law not founded upon absolutes is very dangerous to society. Consider that without absolutes, the Supreme Court has reversed itself over 100 separate times![27]

Judicial "standards now change as rapidly as the Justices. This causes an uncertainty for society; and, in fact, often establishes a dubious standard which, in effect, is no standard at all."[28] Unlike the Bible, the Constitution

26

is not an infallible standard. Returning to a more "pure" constitutionalism is *not* the answer. The answer is found in returning to Yahweh's morality as found in His perfect laws.

The Unbiblical Jury System

Article 3's provision for juries is yet another instance of the framers' deciding they knew better than Yahweh. The Bible offers nothing that resembles a jury system.

Most Constitutionalists favor the jury system, provided jury nullification (a jury's right to judge a law as unjust, oppressive, or inapplicable to any particular case) is in force. However, even if jury nullification were restored, juries would still render decisions based upon each jury's collective standard of morality or immorality. "A jury drawn from the [Biblically] uninstructed population is no better equipped to administer the just requirements of God's law than a corrupt judge."[29] A jury awarded $2.3 million to Stella Liebeck when she burned herself with McDonald's coffee, and a jury found O.J. Simpson innocent on all charges. Although it might be argued that it only takes one juror to dissent and prevent a "railroad job," most people lack the independence and resolution to resist the will of a majority. More often than not, today's jurors reflect the type of people we are warned against in Exodus 23:

> Thou shalt not follow a multitude to do evil; neither shalt thou speak in a cause to decline after many to wrest judgment.
>
> Exodus 23:2

Juries produce, at best, erratic justice. Without Yahweh's laws as the standard, jury decisions are based upon the capricious morality of its members. Nothing demonstrates this better than Jesus' trial by a jury of His peers with Pilate presiding. The prevailing immorality of the day demanded He be crucified even though He was innocent.

> The character of the courts, judges, and legal system cannot be long maintained if the character of the people is delinquent and degenerate. Courts and judges do not exist in a vacuum: they are part of the faith, culture, and moral standards of the people at large, of the nation of which they are a part.[30]

27

Biblical Judges

Although the following passages provide for judges and officers, the Bible nowhere mentions juries:

> For all manner of trespass ... the cause of both parties shall come before the judges....
>
> Exodus 22:9

> Judges and officers shalt thou make thee in all thy gates ... and they shall judge the people with just judgment.
>
> Deuteronomy 16:18

When a judicial system is governed by Biblically qualified judges – whose decisions are based upon Yahweh's commandments, statutes, and judgments – juries are unnecessary. Under such a system, all judicial decisions reflect Yahweh's never-changing morality. Today's unbiblical judges create laws based upon their own values, and these rulings become the binding precedents, called case law, that compel juries to render decisions accordingly:

> There is no crueler tyranny than that which is exercised under cover of law, and with the color of justice....[31]

Christian Courts

Because the situation was similar in first-century Rome, the Apostle Paul admonished Christians to set up their own courts of law:

> Dare any of you, having a matter against another, go to law before the unjust, and not before the saints? Do ye not know that the saints shall judge the world? And if the world shall be judged by you, are ye unworthy to judge the smallest matters? Know ye not that we shall judge angels? How much more things that pertain to this life?... Is it so, that there is not a wise man among you? No, not one that shall be able to judge between his brethren?
>
> 1 Corinthians 6:1-5

Anything less than a Christian court system, governed by Yahweh's commandments, statutes, and judgments, and adjudicated by Biblically qualified judges, fails Paul's criteria. The courts Paul described were to begin with Christians judging Christians, with the objective of someday judging the world.

Modern Christianity has ignored these instructions, content to let non-Christians and even antichrists rule and administer unrighteous judgments. Christianity has become saltless and good for nothing but to be trampled under the foot of man, which, among other things, means being judged by man's standards in man's courts. This is precisely the opposite of what we find described by Solomon: "The evil bow before the good; and the wicked at the gates [where court was convened] of the righteous." (Proverbs 14:19)

At an earlier time in America, Christendom controlled the body politic and administered Yahweh's judgments. The Colony of New Haven, Connecticut, used 1 Corinthians 6:1 and 6:6-7, to justify doing so. Leonard Bacon (1802-1881) wrote the following concerning New Haven's (1639) judicial system:

> Notice ... how great a change, in respect to the inflicting of capital punishments was made by adopting the Hebrew laws, instead of the laws of England. By the laws of England, more than one hundred and fifty crimes were till quite lately, punishable with death. By the laws which the New England colonists adopted, this bloody catalogue was reduced to eleven [murder, treason, perjury against the life of another, kidnapping, bestiality, sodomy, adultery, blasphemy in the highest degree, idolatry, witchcraft, and rebellion against parents].... The greatest and boldest improvement which has been made in criminal jurisprudence, by any one act, since the dark ages, was that which was made by our [colonial] fathers, when they determined, "that the judicial laws of God, as they were delivered by Moses, and as they are a fence to the moral law ... shall be accounted of moral equity, and generally bind all offenders, and be a rule to all the courts."[32]

If the framers intended the Constitution to represent Yahweh, they would have set up the Judicial Branch to resemble that of the New Haven Colony's. The Judicial Branch provided in Article 3 is not equivalent to that provided in the Bible. It is the consequence of Christianity's neglect and rejection of Romans 13:1-7, 1 Corinthians 6:1-6, 2 Corinthians 10:4-6, and 1 Timothy 1:8-11.

29

Article 6

...This Constitution, and the laws of the United States which shall be made in pursuance thereof; and all treaties made, or which shall be made, under the authority of the United States, shall be the supreme law of the land; and the judges in every state shall be bound thereby, any thing in the constitution or laws of any state to the contrary notwithstanding.

The senators and representatives before-mentioned, and the members of the several state legislatures, and all executive and judicial officers, both of the United States and of the several states shall be bound by oath or affirmation, to support this constitution; but no religious test shall ever be required as a qualification to any office or public trust under the United States.

Supreme Law

The framers were fully cognizant of the word "supreme" and its meaning when they declared the supremacy of the Constitution. In so doing, they made the laws of Yahweh subservient to the laws of WE THE PEOPLE.

Thus have ye made the commandment of God of none effect by your tradition. Ye hypocrites, well did Esaias prophesy of you, saying, This people draweth nigh unto me with their mouth, and honoureth me with their lips; but their heart is far from me. But in vain they do worship me, teaching for doctrines the commandments of men.

Matthew 15:6-9

The framers, and today's leaders and Constitutionalists, pay homage to the traditions and commandments of men as the supreme law of the land. Even the Pharisees of Jesus' day were not so brazen to call their man-made traditions supreme.

Supreme God

> Here is not a transient compact between parties: it is the institution of government by an act of the highest sovereignty; the decree of many who are yet one; their law of laws, inviolably supreme....[33]
> *History of the Formation of the Constitution*, 1885

A supreme law can only come from a supreme being. The claim that the Constitution is the supreme law of the land is another witness to the clandestine assertion in the Preamble that WE THE PEOPLE is the god of the United States government. Accordingly, it becomes the god of anyone today who looks to the Constitution as the supreme law of the land. This "supreme law" is a self-contained legal system:

> Our Constitution is a closed legal ... system that declares itself and the laws made pursuant to it, to be the supreme law of the land, and that is the only law it allows.[34]

What does this say about the numerous Biblical laws in disagreement with the Constitution? Consider the following Supreme Court decision:

> All laws which are repugnant to the Constitution are null and void.
> *Marbury v. Madison* (1803)[35]

If we believe the law of WE THE PEOPLE is supreme, then all law that contravenes the Constitution, *including the Bible*, is null and void.

Not only did the framers claim the Constitution as the supreme law of the land, they also declared all subsequent laws and treaties made under the authority of the United States to be supreme as well. As a result, the treaty made with the Muslims of Tripoli also became a part of the supreme law of the land:

> ...the government of the United States of America is not, in any sense, founded on the Christian religion....
> Treaty with Tripoli, of Barbary, Article 11

David Barton admitted that the Treaty with Tripoli's declaration is factual:

> ...this is not an untrue statement since it is referring to the federal government [as opposed to 18th-century America in general]. Recall that while the Founders themselves openly described America as a Christian nation ..., they did include a constitutional prohibition against a federal establishment [of religion]....[36]

If the federal government is not Christian, what is it? At best, it's non-Christian. At worst, it's antichristian. And regardless – thanks to Amendment 1 – it's polytheistic.

Not only does Article 6 make the Treaty with Tripoli a part of the supreme law of the land, it confers the same supremacy on the Charter of the United Nations:

> The Charter has become "the supreme Law of the Land; and the Judges in every State shall be bound thereby, any Thing in the Constitution or Laws of any State to the Contrary notwithstanding."[37]

Anyone promoting the Constitution is equally obligated to promote the non-Christian declaration in the Treaty with Tripoli and the United Nations Charter.

Infanticide and Sodomy

All laws passed by Congress, including those that legalize infanticide and promote sodomy, are also the supreme law of the land. These laws could never be a part of a government predicated upon Yahweh's laws. Instead of legalizing these and other abominations, Yahweh's law condemns infanticide and sodomy as capital crimes. "Laws" legitimizing infanticide and sodomy are only the tip of the insidious iceberg that Christian Constitutionalists are obligated to honor as part of the supreme law of the land:

> The Constitution is like water poured into a cavern. It levels with current religious thought, including atheism, homosexuality and the murder of the unborn.[38]

33

America *was* founded upon Christian principles and was at one time a predominately Christian nation. But a distinction must be made between 17th-century *America* and the late 18th-century *United States of America.* Because most Constitutionalists regard it as one uninterrupted, continuous history, they use the terms interchangeably. What occurred in the 18th-century United States of America was an undeniable departure from 17th-century America, which, for the most part, was governed by the supreme laws of Yahweh.

Religious Test Oaths

The phrase "no religious test shall ever be required as a qualification to any office or public trust under the United States" can only be understood within the historical context of the States' religious test oaths:

> State constitutions enacted during the war [for independence] commonly required test oaths for holding public office. Only Protestants could hold public office in New Jersey or sit in the legislatures of Georgia, South Carolina, and New Hampshire, and only those professing "the Christian religion" could hold public office in Maryland or serve in high government position in Massachusetts. North Carolina limited public office to those who believed in God, the truth of the Protestant religion, and divine authority of both the Old and New Testaments.... Before taking their seats, Pennsylvania legislators had to declare: "I do believe in one God, the creator and governor of the universe, the rewarder of the good and the punisher of the wicked. And I do acknowledge the Scriptures of the Old and New Testament to be given by Divine inspiration." Delaware went further by requiring all office holders to profess belief in the Trinity and the divine inspiration of the Bible.[39]

Because Article 6 outlaws the *Christian* test oaths required by early State constitutions, it bans all Biblical qualifications, particularly Deuteronomy 17:15:

> Thou shalt in any wise set him king [leader] over thee, whom YHWH thy God shall choose....
>
> Deuteronomy 17:15

Because Article 6 is aggressively antichristian, Christian Constitutionalists seldom discuss it. When they do, their argument goes something like this:

> This [differing religious opinions among the constitutional delegates] led the representatives to guard the states from federal intrusion, preserving the authority of the states to establish their own religious parameters. Let the several states work out religious issues on their own terms. There was no need for the federal government to meddle in an area in which the national government would have no jurisdiction. The prohibition of a religious test "as a qualification to any office or public trust under the United States" applied only to *national* office holders: congressmen, senators, the president, and Supreme Court Justices.[40]

This rationalization sidesteps the problem. Are we to believe that congressional representatives, presidents, and Supreme Court justices on the national level are exempt from the Biblical qualifications for leaders? If anything, such qualifications are more crucial on the national level.

Polytheistic Repercussions

Article 6 not only eliminated Christian qualifications for office holders, it paved the way for Jews, Muslims, Hindus, and atheists to be presidents, congressmen, and judges. It became the initial means by which America was transformed from a monotheistic Christian nation to a polytheistic one.

On both the federal and state levels, Jews[41] were instrumental in the removal of the Christian test oaths, and were the first to reap the rewards of these prohibitions. Article 6 was not only an open defiance of the First Commandment, but an unequivocal contravention of the Apostle Paul's admonition to the Corinthians:

> Be ye not unequally yoked together with unbelievers: for what fellowship hath righteousness with unrighteousness? and what communion hath light with darkness? And what concord hath Christ with Belial? or what part hath he that believeth with an infidel? And what agreement hath the temple of God with idols? for ye are the temple of the living God; as God hath said, I will dwell in them, and walk in them; and I will be their God, and they shall be my

people. Wherefore come out from among them, and be ye separate, saith the Lord, and touch not the unclean thing; and I will receive you, and will be a Father unto you, and ye shall be my sons and daughters, saith the Lord Almighty.

2 Corinthians 6:14-18

As important as Paul's directive is for personal relationships, how much more crucial that it be applied to those who govern others? The ramifications are much greater.

Hear this word that YHWH hath spoken against you…. Can two walk together, except they be agreed?

Amos 3:1-3

Since the ratification of the federal Constitution and the eradication of the States' Christian test oaths, the nation's laws – including America's current legislation concerning capital punishment and infanticide – have reflected Talmudic law[42] more than Biblical law.

In 2 Samuel 23:3, Yahweh declared, "He who rules over men must be just, ruling in the fear of God." The framers did *not* legislate so that men would rule in the fear of Yahweh. They left Yahweh completely out of the document, and, in Article 6, they even provided for Jews, Muslims, Hindus, and atheists to rule in the fear of their gods or the god WE THE PEOPLE. Nothing has transformed the political, legal, religious, spiritual, and moral environment of modern America more powerfully than Article 6 of the Constitution. If you want to know why America is now non-Christian and even antichristian, look to Article 6. This is why the Constitution is the single most important issue facing Christians who hope to reclaim dominion in fulfillment of their New Covenant commission:

For the weapons of our warfare are not of the flesh, but divinely powerful for the destruction of fortresses. We are destroying speculations and every lofty thing raised up against the knowledge of God, and we are taking every thought captive to the obedience of Christ, and we are ready to punish all disobedience, whenever your obedience is complete.

2 Corinthians 10:4-6, NASB

Separation of Church and State

Christian Constitutionalists often point out that the term "separation of church and state" is found in the Constitution of the USSR, not the Constitution of the United States. This is true. Nevertheless, the mandate for separation of church and state is inherent in Article 6 on two levels: 1) The Constitution is declared to be the supreme law of the land, which makes any law (secular or Biblical) contrary to this "supreme law" null and void and non-executable by the Constitutional Republic, 2) Religious qualification for government officials is denied, which prohibits Biblical qualifications:

> ...the elimination of a public oath to uphold the Kingship and Law of Jesus Christ in the civil realm automatically erected an ethical "wall of separation" between the Crown Rights of Christ and the new Federal Government, thereby barring all Christians from ever holding public office from that time forward. The fact that professing, and no doubt many genuine, Christians continued in the new system to hold such offices does not negate this assertion. It only demonstrates the "intellectual schizophrenia" (the term is R. J. Rushdoony's) among Christians that has plagued the church for the last two thousand years....[43]

We may debate the intent of the framers, but we cannot debate the effect. Christendom became merely Christianity – salt that lost its savor, good for nothing but to be trampled under the foot of man. Christians have been under the boot of non-Christians and antichrists ever since 1788. We will continue to be the trampled until finally we throw off the current secular government and erect a government based exclusively upon Yahweh's laws.

AMENDMENT 1

Congress shall make no law respecting an establishment of religion,
or prohibiting the free exercise thereof; or abridging the freedom
of speech or the press; or the right of the people peaceably to
assemble, and to petition the government for a redress of
grievances.

The Bill of Rights

The first Ten Amendments, commonly known as the Bill of Rights,
were a compromise between the constitutional framers and the anti-
federalists who opposed the Constitution as originally framed. In theory,
the Bill of Rights protects, among other things, the "unalienable rights" of
"life, liberty, and the pursuit of happiness." But have life, liberty, and
happiness been advanced since the ratification of the Bill of Rights?

One often hears that the Bill of Rights was based upon God-given
rights. The Scriptures provide no evidence of God-given (or unalienable)
rights. Even life and liberty are not rights, but rather responsibilities from
Yahweh. Of course, rights are much more popular than responsibilities.
Everyone, including the homosexual and the infant murderer, demands
his rights, but few are interested in fulfilling their responsibilities.

The Puritan idea of rights and liberty was quite different from what
the framers had in mind:

> John Winthrop [first governor of Massachusetts Bay Colony] ...
> reminded his fellow-citizens of Massachusetts that a doctrine of
> civil rights [as in the Declaration of Independence and the Bill of
> Rights] which looked to natural or sinful man as its source and
> guardian [as in the Preamble] was actually destructive of that very

liberty which they were seeking to protect. True freedom can never be found in institutions which are under the direction of sinful men, but only in the redemption wrought for man by Jesus Christ. Christ, not man, is the sole source and guarantee of true liberty. This two-fold indictment of the democratic philosophy of government is one of the enduring testimonies to the keen insight which these leaders of Massachusetts Bay had into both the theological and practical aspects of an effective type of government.[44]

For the Puritan, liberty was in no way associated with the doctrine of natural law and natural rights, but found its origin and meaning in that covenant which God had made with his people. Liberty was not a natural right, but a God-given right [responsibility] and privilege to be zealously guarded from despots, to be sure, but also subject to precise biblically-defined limits.[45]

Rushdoony pointed out the sophistry of governments based upon freedom:

....[A] society which makes freedom its primary goal will lose it, because it has made, not responsibility, but freedom from responsibility, its purpose. When freedom is the basic emphasis, it is not responsible speech which is fostered but irresponsible speech. If freedom of press is absolutized, libel will be defended finally as a privilege of freedom, and if free speech is absolutized, slander finally becomes a right. Religious liberty becomes a triumph of irreligion. Tyranny and anarchy take over. Freedom of speech, press, and religion all give way to controls, totalitarian controls. The goal must be God's law-order, in which alone is true liberty.[46]

True liberty is found only in Yahweh's law of liberty:

But whoso looketh into the perfect law of liberty, and continueth therein, he being not a forgetful hearer, but a doer of the work, this man shall be blessed in his deed.

James 1:25

James was not describing some New Covenant law that freed us to do whatever we wish. That kind of freedom is nothing more than baptized humanism, which eventually leads to anarchism, one of the quickest paths to legal slavery. Instead, James described the same perfect law of liberty – Yahweh's commandments, statutes, and judgments – as did King David:

> The law of YHWH is perfect, converting the soul.... Psalm 19:7

> So shall I keep thy law continually for ever and ever. And I will walk at liberty.... Psalm 119:44-45

Forgiveness (liberty from our personal sins) is realized through Jesus' blood-atoning sacrifice and resurrection from the grave. All other liberty is found in the implementation and enforcement of Yahweh's perfect laws of liberty – never in the hollow promises of man-made covenants. Yahweh's grace on the personal level and Yahweh's law on the community level are our only means to true freedom. When either of these is abused, freedom is also abused:

> Whenever freedom is made into the absolute, the result is not freedom but anarchism. Freedom must be under law, or it is not freedom.... Only a law-order which holds to the primacy of God's law can bring forth true freedom, freedom for justice, truth, and godly life. Freedom as an absolute is simply an assertion of man's "right" to be his own god; this means a radical denial of God's law-order. "Freedom" thus is another name for the claim by man to divinity and autonomy. It means that man becomes his own absolute.[47]

There is no such thing as *unalienable rights*; there are only *God-ordained responsibilities*. In many instances, the framers ignored or completely subverted these responsibilities, beginning with their rejection of the First and Second Commandments. The first two Commandments were contravened by the Establishment Clause (an endorsement of polytheism) and breached throughout the remainder of the Constitution, since the First and Second Commandments condemn any law but Yahweh's. As Rushdoony put it:

> To have none other gods, means to have no other law than God's law....[48]

> [Because] His law is the expression of His unchanging nature and righteousness, then to abandon the Biblical law for another law-system is to change gods.[49]

41

It is regrettable Rushdoony could not see this as it applies to the Constitution.

The Freedom *of* Religion

> Real Christianity is never tolerated when all religions are tolerated for it is too rigid. True Christians cannot have any other God before them, and they will be judged for endorsing a supposed equality of other gods with the true God. Thus Christians who believe in the freedom of all religions believe in their own termination.[50]

The framers, while perhaps not rejecting Christianity (and in many instances even seeming to prefer it), rejected a Christian state in favor of a polytheistic one. United States Supreme Court Chief Justice Warren E. Burger declared, "our system encourages pluralism, both political and religious."[51] In *Zorach v. Clausen* (1952), Supreme Court Justice William O. Douglas wrote, "We make room for as wide a variety of beliefs and creeds as the spiritual needs of man deem necessary."[52] Christians mistakenly laud such decisions because they are under the spell of the Constitution and their antinomian* preachers. Although modern courts sometimes abuse certain aspects of the original intent of the framers, the statements of Justices Burger and Douglas are in perfect accord with the framers' intent.

Barton definitively proves that the original intent of the Establishment Clause has been abused by modern courts.[54] But he completely ignores the much more consequential abuse Amendment 1 dealt to the First and Second Commandments. Had 18th-century Americans demanded the laws of Yahweh, the courts' abuse would have never occurred. America's courts would have been Christian, governed exclusively by Yahweh's laws. Constitutionalists, like Barton, disprove their claim that they are only interested in the original intent of the framers when they insist on reading God and Christianity into the Constitution, even though the framers explicitly avoided both in the Constitution itself and in the Federalist Papers. Barton argues from a flawed paradigm. His desire to return to the original intent of Amendment 1 is an argument *against* Yahweh and His Word,

---

*"antinomian ... a person who maintains that Christians are freed from the moral law by virtue of grace and faith." *Random House Webster's College Dictionary*[53]

not for it. If we are truly interested in restoring the Bible and its morality to our courts, schools, and society, we must demand that Yahweh's perfect laws replace the Constitution. Otherwise, we must resign ourselves to more of the same immorality we have experienced since the ratification of the Constitution:

> The modern concept [since 1787] of total toleration is not a valid legal principle but an advocacy of anarchism. Shall all religions be tolerated? But, as we have seen, every religion is a concept of law-order. Total toleration means total permissiveness for every kind of practice: idolatry, adultery, cannibalism, human sacrifice, perversion, and all things else. Such total toleration is neither possible nor desirable.... *To tolerate subversion is itself a subversive activity.*[55]

Authorizing Religion

Although the First Amendment does not allow for establishing *one* religion over another, by eliminating Christianity as the federal government's religion of choice (achieved by Article 6's interdiction against Christian test oaths), Amendment 1 authorized equality for all non-Christian and even antichristian religions. When the Constitution failed to recognize Christian monotheism, it allowed Amendment 1 to fill the void by authorizing pagan polytheism.

Amendment 1 did exactly what the framers proclaimed it could not do: it prohibited the exercise of monotheistic Christianity and established polytheism in its place. This explains the government's double standard regarding Christian and non-Christian religions. For example, court participants entering the United States District Court of Appeals for the Middle District of Alabama must walk by a statue of Themis, the Greek goddess of justice. And yet, on November 18, 2002, this very court ruled that Judge Roy Moore's Ten Commandments Monument violated the First Amendment's Establishment Clause. Despite many Christians' claim of hypocrisy, this was in keeping with the inevitable repercussions of the First Amendment.

In response to the U.S. Supreme Court's verdict in *Engle v. Vitale*, which barred school-sponsored prayer, Dr. Billy Graham declared, "This is another step towards the secularization of the United States.... The framers of our Constitution meant we were to have freedom of religion, not freedom from religion."[56] Tragically, Graham's latter statement has become a mantra. Christians hang their religious hat on Amendment 1, as if some great moral principle is carved therein. They have gotten so caught up in the battle over the misuse of the Establishment Clause – the freedom *from* religion – that they have overlooked the ungodliness intrinsic in the Free Exercise Clause – the freedom *of* religion.

Yahweh's law allows individuals the personal choice to be a Christian or not to be a Christian. His law does not legislate private faith, but it does pass judgment on those who openly worship or propagate faith in other gods.

So-called Christians' propensity for defending polytheism is not a modern phenomenon. It was prevalent immediately before, during, and soon after the ratification of the Constitution, as evidenced in many early legislative declarations and judicial decisions. Some judges went so far as to *attribute* the freedom of religion, or polytheism, to Christianity:

> What gave to us this noble safeguard of religious toleration? It was Christianity.
> *City of Charleston v. S.A. Benjamin* (1846)[57]

Barton appeared to relish and even promote this heresy:

> In view of the *Charleston* court, Christian principles had produced America's toleration for other religions; and while America did legislate according to Christian standards of conduct for social behavior, it did not tell other religions how, where, when, or even whether to worship. The only restraints placed on those religions were that their religious practices not be licentious or subversive of public morality or safety. Aside from these stipulations, America granted broad religious toleration to other religions not in spite of, but because of its Christian beliefs.[58]

If Congress were legislating and the judiciary were adjudicating according to Christian standards, they would have never tolerated other religions. Barton continued:

> The court [*Lindenmuller v. the People*, 1860, Supreme Court of New York] further explained that maintaining an official respect for Christianity did not infringe upon the free exercise of religion

for others; instead, it provided an umbrella of protection: "Religious tolerance is entirely consistent with a recognized religion. Christianity may be conceded to be [the] established religion to the qualified extent mentioned, while perfect civil and political equality with freedom of conscience and religious preference is secured to individuals of every other creed and profession...."[59]

Like Rome, post-1791 America is tolerant of all religions that remain subservient to the mother god WE THE PEOPLE. Unlike post-1791 America, 1st-century Christendom stood opposed to Rome and her polytheistic predisposition:

> ...they drew Jason and certain brethren unto the rulers of the city, crying, These that have turned the world upside down are come hither also ... and these all do contrary to the decrees of Caesar, saying that there is another king, one Jesus. Acts 17:6-7

Genuine Christians stand opposed to the Constitution for the same reason.

Amendment 2

A well-regulated militia being necessary to the security of a free state, the right of the people to keep and bear arms shall not be infringed.

Authority

Few Americans are more strident about their constitutional rights, particularly the Second Amendment guarantee to keep and bear arms, than are hunters and gun enthusiasts. Some of the most powerful Washington special-interest groups are organizations (such as the National Rifle Association and Gun Owners of America) formed to protect these rights. As a gun owner and hunter, I am very concerned about my "right" to keep and bear arms. However, as the Christian head of my home, I am much more concerned about my God-ordained *responsibility* to keep and bear arms for the protection of my family, home, and possessions. I am *not* a Second Amendment advocate. Americans who tout the Second Amendment as their authority to keep and bear arms may ultimately do more harm than good to their so-called right.

Because this is a "right" codified by the Constitutional Republic, and thereby brought under its jurisdiction, the Constitutional Republic can divest its citizens of this right – something it has been doing incrementally for some time. On June 26, 2008, in *District of Columbia v. Heller*, 554 U.S., the Supreme Court decided, five to four, that the Second Amendment protects an individual's right to own and bear firearms. Although gun owners hailed *Heller* a victory, this battle (which is far from over) concerning the *constitutional right* to bear arms has diverted our attention from the larger and more consequential battle.

Disconcerting as many Americans may find the erosion of the Second Amendment guarantee, what is even more disturbing is that five people have the power to decide whether United States citizens have the right to protect themselves and their families, to what degree, and with what weapons. The Supreme Court has ruled that Americans have the right to bear arms, *but only until they say otherwise.* Many Americans who celebrated *Heller* overlooked the fact that it can – and likely will – be overturned by a future court, just as its decision overturned *United States v. Miller*, 307 U.S. 174, rendered in 1939. If you look to the Second Amendment for your authority to bear arms, that authority is contingent upon the fickle nature of nine fallible human beings.

On the other hand, because the *responsibility* to keep and bear arms *is* God-given, no one except Yahweh has the right to withdraw or limit their use. If you are a Christian (and particularly if you are the head of your home), you were given the responsibility to keep and bear arms long before the ratification of the Constitution:

> Let the high praises of God be in their mouth, and a two-edged sword in their hand; to execute vengeance upon the heathen, and punishments upon the people; to bind their kings with chains, and their nobles with fetters of iron; to execute upon them the judgment written: this honour have all his saints. Praise ye YH.
>
> Psalm 149:6-9

Constitutionalists often point out that the Second Amendment was added to deter and protect individuals from tyrannous governments. Why do Christian men need the Second Amendment to provide this entitlement when they already have Psalm 149 – unless, of course, they regard Yahweh impotent and His laws inept?

Firearms: Biblically Defended
Self-Defense

Because most of today's pulpits are filled with antinomian, pacifistic, anti-gun pastors, the majority of today's Christians are unaware Yahweh has ordered His disciples to arm themselves. Consequently, Christians have looked to the Second Amendment for their authority to keep and bear arms. Had they been following Paul's instructions in 2 Timothy 2:15 ("Study to shew thyself approved unto God, a workman that needeth not to be ashamed, rightly dividing the word of truth") instead of relying on such pastors, they would have found their authority in the Bible. The question regarding firearms is one of self-defense:

> If the thief is caught while breaking in, and is struck so that he dies, there will be no bloodguiltiness on his account. But if the sun has risen on him, there will be bloodguiltiness on his account.
>
> Exodus 22:2-3, NASB

The crime described in this passage is not theft, but burglary. *Bouvier's Law Dictonary* defines burglary:

> The breaking and entering the house of another in the night-time, with intent to commit a felony therein, whether the felony be actually committed or not.[60]

A person who defends his family, home, or possessions by killing a thief in the dark of the night is not to be held accountable for murder. However, if an unarmed thief who has no intent to cause bodily harm is killed during daylight hours, the killer is to be held responsible for the thief's death. Although unstated, the obvious reason for this distinction is the impossibility of determining an intruder's intentions in the dark of the night. During a night raid, Yahweh gives the benefit of doubt to the home or business owner. The same would be true during the daytime if an assailant's intentions are dubious.

Because Yahweh's law clearly provides for self-defense, our Savior was also a proponent of self-defense:

> …if the head of the house had known at what time of the night the thief was coming, he would have been on the alert and would not have allowed his house to be broken into. Matthew 24:43, NASB

> When a strong man, fully armed, guards his own homestead, his possessions are undisturbed. Luke 11:21, NASB

The better armed we are, the less likely someone will steal from us or harm us and our families. Jesus commanded His disciples to purchase weapons:

> Then said he unto them … he that hath no sword, let him sell his garment, and buy one. Luke 22:36

Jesus never told His disciples to register their swords with the government. French statesman Fredrick Bastiat described self-defense as a natural right:

> Each of us has a natural right – from God – to defend his person, his liberty, and his property. These are the three basic requirements of life, and the preservation of any one of them is completely dependent upon the preservation of the other two. For what are our faculties but the extension of our individuality? And what is property but an extension of our faculties?[61]

What Bastiat depicted as a natural right, the Apostle Paul described as a God-ordained responsibility:

> …if any provide not for his own, and specially for those of his own house, he hath denied the faith, and is worse than an infidel.
>
> 1 Timothy 5:8

After providing for his family's spiritual safety, a Christian man's next priority should be providing for his family's physical protection. Food, clothing, and shelter are of little benefit if you are unprepared or unwilling to defend your family against thieves, rapists, and murderers. It is not unchristian to practice self-defense – it is unchristian if you do *not*.

Defense of Others

Abraham and Moses provide Biblical precedents for taking the law into your own hands to thwart a capital crime. In Genesis 14, Abraham killed in order to rescue his nephew Lot from his kidnappers. In Exodus 2, Moses slew an Egyptian taskmaster who was assaulting a fellow Israelite. Vigilantism is Biblically required[62] when defending or rescuing another person:

> If the bystander has an obligation to render aid "with all lost things" of another man [Deuteronomy 22:1-3], he has an even more pressing obligation to help rescue the man. Thus, this principle of responsibility appears in Deuteronomy 22:24. A woman assaulted in a city is presumed to have given consent if she does not raise a cry, the origin of the hue and cry common law. At her cry, every man within sound of her voice has a duty to render immediate aid….[63]

An eyewitness to a crime has an obligation to the victim and to society to intervene and stop the perpetrator. How many crimes would be averted if thieves, rapists, and murderers knew every Christian man would do whatever necessary to stop them? How much more so, if every law-abiding man also carried a firearm, as per Psalm 149 and Luke 22, for his own protection and the protection of his family and neighbors? Armed citizens are much more likely to intervene and arrest lawbreakers than are those who are unarmed. In cities such as Kennesaw, Georgia, where every household is required by law to possess a firearm, the need for police protection is all but eliminated. A gun in the hand is better than a cop on the phone.

Where Does *Your* Authority Come From?

> Now there was no [black]smith found throughout all the land of Israel: for the Philistines said, Lest the Hebrews make them swords or spears: But all the Israelites went down to the Philistines, to sharpen every man his [plow]share, and his coulter, and his axe, and his mattock.... So it came to pass in the day of battle, that there was neither sword nor spear found in the hand of any of the people that were with Saul and Jonathan....
>
> 1 Samuel 13:19-22

The effort to deprive us of our arms has been with us from nearly the beginning of time. It is imperative we understand the authority to arm ourselves comes from Yahweh. Nearly all gun enthusiasts point to the Second Amendment as their authority for possessing firearms, which means their authority to keep and bear arms can be traced back to 1791. Where did the men living in America *prior* to 1791 get their authority to be armed? I suspect they got it from Exodus 22:2-3; Deuteronomy 22:23-24; Psalm 149:6-9; Luke 11:21, 12:39, 22:36; and 1 Timothy 5:8. Carrying a weapon was already lawful by Yahweh's standards, so why, in 1791, did we need the authorization of the Second Amendment?

If your authority to keep and bear arms is derived from the Second Amendment – from the god WE THE PEOPLE – it is unlikely you will react any differently from the British and Australians who surrendered their weapons when required to do so by their respective governments. On the other hand, if your faith is in Yahweh's sovereign authority, you will be far less likely to turn over your weapons to any civil government un-authorized by the omnipotent Supreme Ruler of the universe.

AMENDMENT 8

Excessive bail shall not be required, nor excessive fines imposed, nor cruel and unusual punishments inflicted.

Cruel and Unusual Punishments

Amendment 8's prohibition against cruel and unusual punishments implies the Constitutional Republic's punishments must be kind and usual. The Constitution's failure to define "cruel and unusual" allows unbiblical and antinomian courts to arbitrarily determine what is allowable.

Capital Punishment

According to the Bible, capital punishment for capital crimes is justifiable homicide.[64] Former Florida attorney general Robert L. Shevin succinctly presented the case for capital punishment:

> The human capacity for good and for compassion makes the death penalty tragic; the human capacity for evil and depraved behavior makes the death penalty necessary.[65]

Leviticus 24:17 and other passages dictate that the judgment for intentional, premeditated murder is death. Human life is so valuable to Yahweh that any man (or animal) that maliciously takes a person's life is to be put to death. Death penalty opponents find this incongruent. They believe life is so valuable it must be protected at all costs. However, the anti-capital punishment proponents are the ones who cheapen life. For example, if a murderer is given twenty years in prison instead of being put to death, the life of the victim has been assigned a value of only twenty years. The life of a murderer is certainly not more valuable than the life of the person he murdered. Put another way, the life of the person murdered is *so* valuable it requires the life of the murderer:

> ...surely your blood of your lives will I require; at the hand of every beast will I require it, and at the hand of man; at the hand of every man's brother will I require the life of man. Whoso sheddeth man's blood, by man shall his blood be shed: for in the image of God made he man.
>
> Genesis 9:5-6

Premeditated murder is the one crime for which Yahweh offers no civil clemency:

> ...ye shall take no satisfaction [restitution] for the life of a murderer, which is guilty of death: but he shall be surely put to death. And ye shall take no satisfaction for him [the convicted murderer].... So ye shall not pollute the land wherein ye are: for blood it defileth the land: and the land cannot be cleansed of the blood that is shed therein, but by the blood of him that shed it.
>
> Numbers 35:31-33

Because Yahweh is a loving and merciful God, who desires no one to perish and everyone to come to repentance, His judgments are not only just, but also remedial and preventative:

> And thou shalt stone him [a promoter of false gods] with stones, that he die; because he hath sought to thrust thee away from YHWH thy God.... And all Israel shall hear, and fear, and shall do no more any such wickedness as this is among you.
>
> Deuteronomy 13:10-11

Yahweh instituted capital punishment as a deterrent to criminal behavior:

> The death penalty ... provides a deterrence effect – deterring the criminal from future crime (he dies), deterring other criminals from committing similar crimes (fear of death), and deterring God from bringing His covenant judgments on the community for its failure to uphold covenant law (fear of God's wrath).[66]

Ronald L. Dart and Philip G. Kayser, respectively, provide the following compelling statistics:

> Of all the men currently in prison ... how many of these men had been tried and convicted of murder, had been released, and then had killed again? The number ran to more than eight hundred.... Five of these killers had not been released, but had killed prison guards. Whatever our academic arguments about deterrence and

the death penalty, here is something we have to deal with. There are eight hundred citizens and five prison guards who would still be alive today if these killers had been quickly dispatched.[67]

...from the time that the death penalty was once again legal in America (1977) to February of 2007 there have only been 1137 executions. Yet the period of time has had well over half a million murders.[68]

Opponents of the death penalty believe any form of capital punishment is inhumane, and even the champions of capital punishment are always seeking a more humane means of execution. They claim to be motivated by mercy and compassion. Mercy and compassion for whom? Certainly not for the victims, the victims' next of kin, society, or latent criminals. Who does this leave except the convicted criminals? Unrepentant murderers, rapists, and other capital felons do not deserve our compassion and mercy. To show mercy to such criminals implies we believe we are more virtuous than Yahweh. Although death penalty opponents see themselves as merciful and kind, in truth they are cruel to everyone *but* the criminal. In Proverbs 12:10, Solomon wrote, "the tender mercies of the wicked are cruel."

Christians today are afraid of the laws of the Bible. They are actually embarrassed by them. They do not recognize that biblical law is a two-edged sword of God's judgment: blessing for the righteous, but cursing for the unrighteous (Rom. 13:1-7). They do not understand that God's law-order for society is merciful. For example, God requires the death penalty for kidnappers (Ex. 21:16). The death penalty used to be imposed on kidnappers in the United States, and kidnapping was rare. It is no longer imposed regularly, and kidnapping has become a blight. Kidnapping by terrorists in Europe is commonplace. Who says that God's law regarding kidnapping is too harsh? Harsher than kidnapping itself? So it is with all of God's civil laws [and their judgments]. They are merciful compared with the effects of unpunished evil. The modern world is learning just how unmerciful a society can be that is not governed by biblical law.[69]

The purpose of capital punishment is to remove the criminal from society and cleanse the community of evil, which, in turn, provides for peace and security and a well-ordered society. Fewer criminals and fewer victims are the obvious benefits of such a policy.

In order for the death penalty to be the greatest possible deterrent, Yahweh chose a brutal form of execution. The harsher the punishment, the greater the deterrent. People are less likely to write checks against insufficient funds when they are penalized thirty dollars rather than thirty cents. Likewise, people are less likely to commit felonies when the maximum penalty is mandatory for unrepentant criminals. This is especially true if it is compulsory for the whole community to attend and participate in public punishments:

> And YHWH spake unto Moses, saying, Bring forth him that hath cursed without the camp; and let all that heard him lay their hands upon his head, and let all the congregation [community] stone him.... And he that blasphemeth the name of YHWH, he shall surely be put to death, and all the congregation shall certainly stone him: as well the stranger, as he that is born in the land....
> Leviticus 24:13-16

Some people's "sense of decency" pits them against Yahweh's righteous judgments. Anyone who prefers to show mercy to a convicted criminal, rather than assuring greater public safety, is only concerned about protecting his own sensibilities and making himself feel good.

Christian Fear of Judgments

> Run ye to and fro ... and see now, and know, and seek in the broad places thereof, if ye can find a man, if there be any that executeth judgment, that seeketh the truth....
> Jeremiah 5:1

Every viable, dynamic law contains three integral components: commandments, statutes, and judgments:

> ...he [Yahweh] declared unto you his covenant [law], which he commanded you to perform, even ten commandments.... And YHWH commanded me [Moses] at that time to teach you statutes and judgments, that ye might do them in the land whither ye go over to possess it.
> Deuteronomy 4:13-14

Without any one of these three components, the law is crippled. For example, modern society has initiated traffic laws, including regulations against speeding. However, without statutes to explain what constitutes speeding in each particular situation (e.g., an excess of 20 mph in a school zone), the commandment cannot be fully understood or obeyed. Without judgments, the law has no teeth with which to check potential transgressors.

Those who render the judgments hold dominion in society. That Yahweh intends for the judgments to be in the hands of His people is unmistakable:

> Let ... a two-edged sword [be] in their hand; to execute vengeance upon the heathen, and punishments upon the people; to bind their kings with chains, and their nobles with fetters of iron; to execute upon them the judgment written: this honour have all his saints. Praise ye YH.
>
> Psalm 149:6-9

Even most so-called pronomians abdicate one third of Yahweh's law – the judgments – to the non-Christians. Those who define criminal behavior and dispense judgment clearly rule society. Antinomians' aversion to Yahweh's judgments can only mean they believe man's judgments are superior to Yahweh's and that non-Christians are more competent to dispense judgment than Christians, which in turn means most modern Christians do not believe "...the judgments of YHWH are true and righteous altogether" (Psalm 19:9). They also do not believe "the law of YHWH is perfect" (Psalm 19:7), because any law void of its judgments is an imperfect law, lacking one third of its indispensable components. To abolish a Commandment's judgment is to gut the Commandment the judgment enforces:

> There has been an ancient tradition on the part of Christian commentators of appealing selectively to Old Testament laws whenever convenient in moral arguments, but almost never to the God specified sanctions.... This is wholly illegitimate exegetically, and it has led to the accusation by consistent critics that Christians who uphold "the moral law of God" apart from God's specified civil sanctions are hypocritical, that they want all the moral benefits of theocracy without any of the embarrassing theocratic sanctions.[70]

Antinomian author Roy L. Aldrich makes this very point:

> If the Ten Commandments of the law are still binding then all of the penalties must remain the same. The death penalties should be

imposed for Sabbath-breaking, idolatry, adultery, rebellion against parents, etc. To change the penalty of a law means to abolish that law. A law without a penalty is an anomaly. A law with its penalty abolished becomes only good advice.[71]

North clearly depicts the problem:

The modern church simply pays no attention to God's ecclesiastical sanctions. Therefore, pagans pay very little attention to the churches. Why should they? The church is like an army without hierarchical order and without sanctions against mutiny. Such an army cannot win a battle. Pagans instinctively recognize this; Christians may also sense it, but then they blame eschatology rather than their own judicial cowardice.[72]

Those opposed to Yahweh's judgments prefer crime over judgment, criminals over the innocent, and man's laws – at least man's judgments – over Yahweh's. Put another way, they would prefer people be murdered, kidnapped, raped, and plundered rather than claim responsibility for administering Yahweh's righteous judgments.

Despite most pronomians' strong belief in capital punishment, they ironically relinquish to the heathen the determination for what should and should not be capital offenses. History indicates their dereliction of duty may one day result in the deaths of their children or grandchildren for proclaiming Jesus as Lord and Savior.

Christians who prefer Amendment 8 over Psalm 19:9 are guilty of the same sin as Job:

Wilt thou also disannul my [Yahweh's] judgment? Wilt thou condemn me, that thou mayest be righteous?

Job 40:8

In order to return to Yahweh, we must return to His law, including His righteous judgments:

…judgment shall return unto righteousness: and all the upright in heart shall follow it. Who will rise up for me against the evildoers? Or who will stand up for me against the workers of iniquity?

Psalm 94:15-16

If Christians hope to regain dominion, they must be prepared not only to implement Yahweh's commandments and statutes, but also to enforce His judgments. Otherwise, we will continue to face the consequences:

[You have] ... changed my judgments into wickedness ... for they have refused my judgments and my statutes, they have not walked in them. Therefore thus saith the Lord YHWH; Because ye ... have not walked in my statutes, neither have kept my judgments ... behold, I, even I, am against thee, and will execute judgments in the midst of thee in the sight of the nations.

Ezekiel 5:6-8

Conclusion
The Dualism of "Christian" Constitutionalists

Yahweh has a monopoly on sovereignty, justice, and legislation (Isaiah 33:22). Although Christian Constitutionalists may claim they believe this affirmation, in practice, they reject Yahweh as King, Judge, and Lawgiver, just as the Israelites did when they chose a flesh and blood king instead of Yahweh. They are like the Babylonian King Nebuchadnezzar who, on one hand, proclaimed Yahweh as the God of gods and, on the other hand, erected an image made in his own likeness. What is interesting about this dualism is that most people do not realize they are afflicted with it. Aaron apparently did not realize he was practicing dualism when, in Exodus 32:3-5, he dubbed the golden calf "Yahweh." A Christian's devotion cannot be split between Yahweh's perfect law and man's law:

> How long halt ye between two opinions? If YHWH be God, follow him: but if Baal, then follow him.   1 Kings 18:21

> No man can serve two masters: for either he will hate the one, and love the other; or else he will hold to the one, and despise the other. Ye cannot serve God and mammon.   Matthew 6:24

The claim of Christian Constitutionalism is oxymoronic. It is spiritual schizophrenia. As Christians, and therefore subjects of the King of kings, our devotion is due *exclusively* to Yahweh and His kingdom and laws. Synonyms of devotion include fidelity, allegiance, ardor, fealty, loyalty, and homage. These are all forms of worship to which Yahweh claims exclusive rights:

> Israel is an empty vine, he bringeth forth fruit unto himself: according to the multitude of his fruit he hath increased the altars [to idols]; according to the goodness of his land they have made goodly images [sacred pillars, NASB]. Their heart is divided; now

shall they be found faulty.... For now they shall say, We have no king, because we feared not YHWH....

Hosea 10:1-3

Yahweh declared Israel was bringing forth fruit unto themselves. Is this not what "a government of, by, and for the people" does? When Christians appeal to both the Bible and a Constitution that is antithetical and antagonistic to Yahweh's laws, how can their hearts not be divided? They no more serve Yahweh as their King than did the Israelites in Hosea's day:

> ...the Assyrian shall be his king, because they refused to return. And the sword shall abide on his cities, and shall consume his branches, and devour them, because of their own counsels [because they do what they themselves think best, TEV]. And my people are bent to backsliding from me: though they called them to the most High, none at all would exalt him.

Hosea 11:5-7

Our loyalty is due only to Yahweh and His law. His battle, and thus His subjects' battle, is not for constitutionalism, but for His kingdom here on earth as it is in heaven, governed solely by His perfect laws.

Cost and Reward

It is time for Christians to stop serving two masters. We must choose between the document that begins "We the People," and the one that begins "In the beginning God." We must choose between a government of, by, and for the people and a government of, by, and for Yahweh. Like Gideon in Judges 6, we must first tear down our fathers' idol and altar before we can restore Yahweh's kingdom here on earth.

Without question, this is a costly decision. It will, at the very least, demand a change in beliefs. It will cost some people their pride. It will cost relationships, perhaps fellowship, and, for some, even their ministries. People will be persecuted. However, any cost incurred will be far exceeded by the rewards of choosing correctly: Yahweh's pleasure and blessings, the legacy we leave our posterity, peace and prosperity, and the foundations for what will ultimately be the near elimination of crime.

If WE THE PEOPLE be God, follow them. But if Yahweh be God, we *must* follow Him. As for me and my house and everyone who truly believes Yahweh, His kingdom, and His laws are perfect and sufficient – we will follow and serve Yahweh as God, King, Judge, and Lawgiver, in the life to come *and* here on earth now.

END NOTES

1. For a more thorough explanation concerning the sacred names of God, "The Third Commandment" may be read online, or the book *Thou shalt not take the name of YHWH thy God in vain* may be ordered from Mission to Israel Ministries, PO Box 248, Scottsbluff, Nebraska 69363, for a suggested $4 donation.*

2. For a more thorough explanation concerning baptism and its relationship to salvation, the book *Baptism: All You Wanted to Know and More* may be requested from Mission to Israel Ministries, PO Box 248, Scottsbluff, Nebraska 69363, for free.

3. Dennis Oliver Woods, *Discipling the Nations: The Government Upon His Shoulder* (Franklin, TN: Legacy Communications, 1996) p. 82.

4. For a more thorough explanation concerning the use of the names of God, "The Third Commandment" may be read online, or the book *Thou shalt not take the name of YHWH thy God in vain* may be ordered from Mission to Israel Ministries, PO Box 248, Scottsbluff, Nebraska, 69363, for a suggested $4 donation.*

5. John Clark Ridpath, *History of the United States*, 4 vols. (New York, NY: The American Book Company, 1874) vol. 1, p. 181.

6. Gary DeMar and Peter Leithart, *The Reduction of Christianity: A Biblical Response to Dave Hunt* (Ft. Worth, TX: Dominion Press and Atlanta, GA: American Vision, 1988) p. 300.

7. Francis Schaeffer, *A Christian Manifesto* (1981), in *The Complete Works of Francis Schaeffer*, 5 vols. (Wheaton, IL: Crossway Books, 1982) vol. 5, p. 426.

---

*We are admonished in Matthew 10:8 "freely ye have received, freely give." Although we have a suggested price for our books, we do not sell them. In keeping with 2 Corinthians 9:7, this ministry is supported by freewill offerings. If you cannot afford the suggested price, inform us of your situation, and we will be pleased to provide you with whatever you need for whatever you can send.

8. Fundamental Agreement of the Colony of New Haven, Connecticut, 1639, <http://cclce.org/files/ResourceCD/documents/Connecticut/1639_Fundamental_Agreement,_or_Original_Constitution_of_the_Colony_of_New_Haven.html>.

9. James Bruggeman, epilogue to *Christian Duty Under Corrupt Government: A Revolutionary Commentary of Romans 13:1-7*, by Ted R. Weiland, 2nd ed. (Scottsbluff, NE: Mission to Israel Ministries, 2006, 2nd ed.). *Christian Duty Under Corrupt Government* may be ordered from Mission to Israel Ministries, PO Box 248, Scottsbluff, Nebraska 69363, for a suggested $7 donation.*

10. Patrick Henry, Ralph Ketcham, ed., "Speeches of Patrick Henry (June 5 and 7, 1788)," *The Anti-Federalist Papers and the Constitutional Convention Debates* (New York, NY: Penguin Books, 2003, 2nd ed.) pp. 200-08.

11. Johann Wolfgang von Goethe, Otto Wenckstern, trans., *Goethe's Opinions on the World, Mankind, Literature, Science and Art* (London, UK: John W. Parker and Son, 1853) p. 3.

12. For a more thorough explanation concerning the use of the sacred names of God, "The Third Commandment" may be read at missionto israel.org/3rdcom-pt1.php, or *Thou shalt not take the name of YHWH thy God in vain* may be ordered from Mission to Israel Ministries, PO Box 248, Scottsbluff, Nebraska 69363, for a suggested $4 donation.*

13. Noah Webster, *American Dictionary of the English Language*, s.v. "Legislator" (1828; reprint ed. San Francisco, CA: The Foundation for American Christian Education, 1967).

14. W.W. Turner, *The Amazing Story of the British Sovereign* (Nashville, TN: 1970) p. 4, quoted in Rousas John Rushdoony, *The Institutes of Biblical Law* (The Presbyterian and Reformed Publishing Company, 1973) p. 644.

---

*We are admonished in Matthew 10:8 "freely ye have received, freely give." Although we have a suggested price for our books, we do not sell them. In keeping with 2 Corinthians 9:7, this ministry is supported by freewill offerings. If you cannot afford the suggested price, inform us of your situation, and we will be pleased to provide you with whatever you need for whatever you can send.

15. Lysander Spooner, *No Treason, No. VI, The Constitution of No Authority*, <http://praxeology.net/LS-NT-6.htm#.>

16. William Holmes McGuffey, *McGuffey's Sixth Eclectic Reader* (New York, NY: American Book Company, 1879) p. 225.

17. John Locke, *Two Treatises of Government* (London, UK: C. & J. Rivington) p. 211.

18. For a more thorough explanation concerning baptism and its relationship to salvation, the book *Baptism: All You Wanted to Know and More* may be requested from Mission to Israel Ministries, PO Box 248, Scottsbluff, Nebraska 69363, for free.

19. Rousas John Rushdoony, *The Institutes of Biblical Law* (The Presbyterian and Reformed Publishing Company, 1973) p. 613.

20. Ibid., p. 625.

21. Alexis de Tocqueville, *Democracy in America and Two Essays on America* (London, UK: Penguin Books Ltd., 2003) p. 315.

22. Gary North, *Political Polytheism: The Myth of Pluralism* (Tyler, TX: Institute for Christian Economics, 1989) p. 502.

23. Otto Scott, "Easy Chair" audiotape #165 (March 10, 1988) distributed by Chalcedon Foundation, P.O. Box 158, Vallecito, CA 95251, quoted in Gary North, *Political Polytheism: The Myth of Pluralism* (Tyler, TX: Institute for Christian Economics, 1989) p. 675.

24. International Information Programs, USINFO.STATE.GOV, "Religious Liberty in the Modern Era," *Rights of the People: Individual Freedom and the Bill of Rights*, <http://uninfo.state.gov/products/pubs/rightsof/modern.htm>.

25. Chief Justice Warren E. Burger, Introduction, William Swindler, *The Constitution and Chief Justice Marshall* (New York, NY: Dodd, Mead & Company, 1978) p. xiii.

26. James Madison, June 17, 1789, *The Debates and Proceedings in the Congress of the United States* (Washington, DC: Gales and Seaton, 1834) vol. 1, p. 520.

27. Mark A. Beliles, Douglas S. Anderson, *Contending for the Constitution: Recalling the Christian Influence on the Writing of the Constitution and the Biblical Basis of American Law and Liberty* (Charlottesville, VA: Providence Foundation, 2005) p. 146.

28. David Barton, *Original Intent: The Courts, the Constitution, & Religion* (Aledo, TX: WallBuilder Press, 4th Edition, 1st Printing, February 2005) p. 233.

29. Dennis Oliver Woods, *A Handbook of Biblical Law* (Prepublication, 2010) p. 12.

30. Rushdoony, p. 639.

31. *U.S. v. Jannotti*, 673 F.2d 578, 614 (3d Cir. 1982).

32. Leonard Bacon, *Thirteen Historical Discourses, on the Completion of Two Hundred Years, From the Beginning of the First Church in New Haven, With an Appendix* (New Haven, CT: Durrie & Peck, 1839) p. 32.

33. George Bancroft, *History of the Formation of the Constitution*, 5 vols. (New York, NY: D. Appleton and Company, 1885) vol. 3, p. 357.

34. Thomas James Norton, *The Constitution of the United States, Its Sources and Its Application*, circa 1922, <http://www.barefootsworld.net/constit1.html>.

35. *Marbury v. Madison*, 5 US (2 Cranch) 137, 164, 176 (1803).

36. Barton, p. 127.

37. *Sei Fujii v. the State of California*, "Opinion of the District Court of Appeal, Second District, Division 2, California, April 24, 1952," in United States Congress, Senate Committee on Foreign Relations, *Review of the United Nations Charter: Report of the Subcommittee on the United Nations Charter, pursuant to the provisions of the 83rd Congress, 2d Session Senate Document No. 87 – Subcommittee on the United Nations Charter Pursuant to S. Res. 126, 83rd Congress, 1st Session ... April 23, 1956*, p. 288.

38. John Spencer, *The Constitution of the United States: A Man Inspired Document!*, p. 4.

39. Arlin M. Adams and Charles J. Emmerich, *A Nation Dedicated to Religious Liberty: The Constitutional Heritage of the Religious Clauses* (Philadelphia, PA: University of Pennsylvania Press, 1990) p. 14.

40. Gary DeMar, "God and the Constitution," 4 November 2005, <http://www.americanvision.org/article/god-and-the-constitution/>.

41. Today's Jewish people are known as Jews not because of physical descent from Abraham, Isaac, and Jacob, but because their Khazarian predecessors adopted the religion of Judaism (Talmudism) between the seventh and ninth centuries A.D. For a more thorough explanation regarding the identity of today's Jews, *God's Covenant People: Yesterday, Today and Forever* may be read at missiontoisrael.org/gods-covenant-people/tableofcontents.php, or the book may be ordered from Mission to Israel Ministries, PO Box 248, Scottsbluff, Nebraska 69363, for a suggested $14 donation.*

42. For documentation regarding the heretical nature of the Babylonian Talmud, *God's Covenant People: Yesterday, Today and Forever* may be read at missiontoisrael.org/gods-covenant-people/tableofcontents.php, or the book may be ordered from Mission to Israel Ministries, PO Box 248, Scottsbluff, Nebraska 69363, for a suggested $14 donation.*

43. Greg Loren Durand, "An Oath is an Act of Worship," *The U.S. Constitution – America's Covenantal Apostasy* (Dahlonega, GA: Crown Rights Book Company) p. 4.

44. C. Gregg Singer, *A Theological Interpretation of American History* (Phillipsburg, NJ: Presbyterian and Reformed Publishing Co., 1964) p. 19.

45. Ibid., p. 17.

46. Rushdoony, p. 581.

47. Ibid., p. 583.

---

*We are admonished in Matthew 10:8 "freely ye have received, freely give." Although we have a suggested price for our books, we do not sell them. In keeping with 2 Corinthians 9:7, this ministry is supported by freewill offerings. If you cannot afford the suggested price, inform us of your situation, and we will be pleased to provide you with whatever you need for whatever you can send.

48. Ibid., p. 47.

49. Ibid., p. 20.

50. Dr. H. Rondel Rumburg, Foreword (21 February 1998) to Dr. Robert L. Dabney, *Anti-Biblical Theories of Rights*, which first appeared in the *Presbyterian Quarterly*, July 1888, (Hueytown, AL: Society for Biblical and Southern Studies, 1998) p. 6.

51. Warren E. Burger, Foreword, Arlin M. Adams, Charles J. Emmerich, *A Nation Dedicated to Religious Liberty: The Constitutional Heritage of the Religion Clauses* (Philadelphia, PA: University of Pennsylvania Press, 1990) p. xiv.

52. William O. Douglas, *Zorach v. Clausen*, 343 U.S. 306 (1952).

53. *Random House Webster's College Dictionary*, "antinomian" (New York, NY: Random House, 2000) p. 59.

54. David Barton, *Original Intent: The Courts, the Constitution, & Religion* (Aledo, TX: WallBuilder Press, 4th Edition, 1st Printing, February 2005).

55. Rushdoony, p. 89.

56. Dr. Billy Graham, quoted in Leo Pfeffer, *God, Caesar, and The Constitution: The Court as Referee of Church-State Confrontation* (Boston, MA: Beacon Press, 1975) p. 40.

57. *City of Charleston v. S.A. Benjamin*, 2 Strob. 521-524 (1846), South Carolina Supreme Court.

58. Barton, p. 70.

59. Ibid., p. 71.

60. John Bouvier, "Burglary," *Bouvier's Law Dictionary: A Concise Encyclopedia of the Law*, 3 vols. (Kansas City, MO: Vernon Law Book Company, 1914) vol. 1, p. 404.

61. Fredrick Bastiat, *The Law* (Irvington-on-Hudson, NY: The Foundation for Economic Education, Inc., [1848] 1987) p. 6.

62. For a study on *unlawful* vigilantism, the book *The Phinehas Hoods: A Biblical Examination of Unscriptural Vigilantism* may be read at missiontoisrael.org/Phinehas-Hoods.php, or the book may be ordered from Mission to Israel Ministries, PO Box 248, Scottsbluff, Nebraska 69363 for a suggested $3 donation.*

63. Rushdoony, p. 464.

64. For a more thorough study on what constitutes lawful and unlawful homicide, "The Sixth Commandment" may be read at missiontoisrael.org/6thcom.php, or the book *Thou shalt not kill* may be ordered from Mission to Israel Ministries, PO Box 248, Scottsbluff, Nebraska 69363, for a suggested $4 donation.*

65. Robert L. Shevin, quoted in International Information Programs, USInfo.org, "Cruel or Unusual Punishment," *Rights of the People: Individual Freedom and the Bill of Rights*, <http://usinfo.org/zhtw/DOCS/RightsPeople/punish.html>.

66. Gary North, *Tools of Dominion: The Case Laws of Exodus* (Tyler, TX: The Institute for Christian Economics, 1990/1997) p. 324.

67. Ronald L. Dart, *Capital Punishment: A Christian Dilemma* (Whitehouse, TX: Christian Educational Ministries, 1998) p. 11.

68. Philip G. Kayser, *Is the Death Penalty Just?* (Omaha, NE: Biblical Blueprints, 2007/2009) p. 31.

69. Gary North, *Political Polytheism: The Myth of Pluralism,* p. 581.

70. Gary North, *Tools of Dominion: The Case Laws of Exodus*, p. 915.

71. Roy L. Aldrich, "Causes for Confusion of Law and Grace," *Bibliotheca Sacra*, vol. 116 (July 1959) p. 226, quoted in Gary North, *Tools of Dominion: The Case Laws of Exodus* (Tyler, TX: The Institute for Christian Economics, 1997) pp. 913-14.

---

*We are admonished in Matthew 10:8 "freely ye have received, freely give." Although we have a suggested price for our books, we do not sell them. In keeping with 2 Corinthians 9:7, this ministry is supported by freewill offerings. If you cannot afford the suggested price, inform us of your situation, and we will be pleased to provide you with whatever you need for whatever you can send.

72. Gary North, *Political Polytheism: The Myth of Pluralism*, p. 600.

BIBLIOGRAPHY

Adams, Arlin M., and Emmerich, Charles J. *A Nation Dedicated to Religious Liberty: The Constitutional Heritage of the Religious Clauses.* Philadelphia, PA: University of Pennsylvania Press, 1990.

Aldrich, Roy L. "Causes for Confusion of Law and Grace," *Bibliotheca Sacra*, vol. 116 (July 1959), 1997.

Bacon, Leonard. *Thirteen Historical Discourses, on the Completion of Two Hundred Years, From the Beginning of the First Church in New Haven, With an Appendix.* New Haven, CT: Durrie & Peck, 1839.

Bancroft, George. *History of the Formation of the Constitution.* New York, NY: D. Appleton and Company, 1885.

Barton, David. *Original Intent: The Courts, the Constitution, & Religion.* Aledo, TX: WallBuilder Press, 2005.

Bastiat, Fredrick. *The Law.* Irvington-on-Hudson, NY: The Foundation for Economic Education, Inc., [1848] 1987.

Beliles, Mark A., and Anderson, Douglas S. *Contending for the Constitution: Recalling the Christian Influence on the Writing of the Constitution and the Biblical Basis of American Law and Liberty.* Charlottesville, VA: Providence Foundation, 2005.

Bouvier, John. *Bouvier's Law Dictionary: A Concise Encyclopedia of the Law.* Kansas City, MO: Vernon Law Book Company, 1914.

Bruggeman, James. Epilogue to *Christian Duty Under Corrupt Government: A Revolutionary Commentary of Romans 13:1-7* by Ted R. Weiland. Scottsbluff, NE: Mission to Israel Ministries, 2006.

Burger, Chief Justice Warren E. Foreword to *A Nation Dedicated to Religious Liberty: The Constitutional Heritage of the Religion Clauses* by Arlin M. Adams, and Charles J. Emmerich. Philadelphia, Pa: University of Pennsylvania Press, 1990.

Burger, Chief Justice Warren E. Introduction to *The Constitution and Chief Justice Marshall* by William Swindler. New York, NY: Dodd, Mead & Company, 1978.

City of Charleston v. S.A. Benjamin. South Carolina Supreme Court. 1846.

Dart, Ronald L. *Capital Punishment: A Christian Dilemma.* Whitehouse, TX: Christian Educational Ministries, 1998.

DeMar, Gary. "God and the Constitution," 4 November 2005, <http://www.americanvision.org/article/god-and-the-constitution/>.

DeMar, Gary, and Leithart, Peter. *The Reduction of Christianity: A Biblical Response to Dave Hunt.* Ft. Worth, TX: Dominion Press and Atlanta, GA: American Vision, 1988.

de Tocqueville, Alexis. *Democracy in America and Two Essays on America.* London, UK: Penguin Books Ltd., 2003.

Douglas, Justice William O. *Zorach v. Clausen,* 1952.

Durand, Greg Loren. *The U.S. Constitution – America's Covenantal Apostasy.* Dahlonega, GA: Crown Rights Book Company.

Fundamental Agreement of the Colony of New Haven, Connecticut. <http://cclce.org/files/ResourceCD/documents/Connecticut/1639_Fundamental_Agreement,_or_Original_Constitution_of_the_Colony_of_New_Haven.html.>

Goethe, Johann Wolfgang von. *Goethe's Opinions on the World, Mankind, Literature, Science and Art.* London, UK: John W. Parker and Son, 1853.

Henry, Patrick. "Speeches of Patrick Henry." June 5 and 7, 1788.

International Information Programs, "Religious Liberty in the Modern Era," *Rights of the People: Individual Freedom and the Bill of Rights,* <http://uninfo.state.gov/products/pubs/rightsof/modern.htm>.

Kayser, Philip G. *Is the Death Penalty Just?* Omaha, NE: Biblical Blueprints, 2007/2009.

Ketcham, Ralph, ed. *The Anti-federalist Papers and the Constitutional Convention Debates.* New York, NY: Penguin Books, 2003.

Locke, John. *Two Treatises of Government*. London: UK: C. & J. Rivington.

Madison, James. *The Debates and Proceedings in the Congress of the United States* (June 17, 1789). Washington, DC: Gales and Seaton, 1834.

Marbury v. Madison. 1803.

McGuffey, William Holmes. *McGuffey's Sixth Eclectic Reader*. New York, NY: American Book Company, 1879.

North, Gary. *Political Polytheism: The Myth of Pluralism*. Tyler, TX: Institute for Christian Economics, 1989.

North, Gary. *Tools of Dominion: The Case Laws of Exodus*. Tyler, TX: The Institute for Christian Economics, 1997.

Norton, Thomas James. *The Constitution of the United States, Its Sources and Its Application*, circa 1922, <http://www.barefootsworld.net/constit1.html>.

Pfeffer, Leo. *God, Caesar, and The Constitution: The Court as Referee of Church-State Confrontation*. Boston, MA: Beacon Press, 1975, quoting Dr. Billy Graham.

Random House Webster's College Dictionary. New York, NY: Random House, 2000.

Ridpath, John Clark, *History of the United States*. New York, NY: The American Book Company, 1874.

Rumburg, Dr. H. Rondel. Foreword (21 February 1998) to *Anti-Biblical Theories of Rights* by Dr. Robert L. Dabney. Hueytown, AL: Society for Biblical and Southern Studies, 1998.

Rushdoony, Rousas John. *The Institutes of Biblical Law*. The Presbyterian and Reformed Publishing Company, 1973.

Schaeffer, Francis. *The Complete Works of Francis Schaeffer*. Wheaton, IL: Crossway Books, 1982.

Scott, Otto. "Easy Chair." No. #165. Vallecito, CA: Chalcedon Foundation, 10 March 1988.

Sei Fujii v. the State of California. 1952.

Shevin, Robert L. Quoted in International Information Programs, USInfo.org, "Cruel or Unusual Punishment," *Rights of the People: Individual Freedom and the Bill of Rights*, <http://usinfo.org/zhtw/ DOCS/RightsPeople/punish.html>.

Singer, C. Gregg. *A Theological Interpretation of American History.* Phillipsburg, NJ: Presbyterian and Reformed Publishing Co., 1964.

Spencer, John. *The Constitution of the United States: A Man Inspired Document!*

Spooner, Lysander. *No Treason, No.VI, The Constitution of No Authority*, <http://praxeology.net/LS-NT-6.htm#.>

Turner, W.W. *The Amazing Story of the British Sovereign.* 1970.

U.S. v. Jannotti. 1982.

Webster, Noah. *American Dictionary of the English Language.* San Francisco, CA: The Foundation for American Christian Education, [1828] 1967.

Woods, Dennis Oliver. *A Handbook of Biblical Law.* Prepublication, 2010.

Woods, Dennis Oliver. *Discipling the Nations: The Government Upon His Shoulder.* Franklin, TN: Legacy Communications, 1996.

Zorach v. Clausen. 1952.

Subject Index

A

Abraham (vigilante), p. 50
Aldrich, Roy L., pp. 57-58
Amendment 1, pp. 3, 39-45
Amendment 2, pp. 3, 47-51
Amendment 8, pp. 3, 53-59
"a more perfect union," p. 9
anarchism/anarchy, pp. 40, 41, 43
anomianism, p. 8
anti-capital punishment
   proponents, p. 53
anti-federalists, pp. 10, 39
anti-gun pastors, p. 48
antinomian aversion to Yahweh's
   judgments, p. 57
antinomian courts, p. 53
appointments, pp. 19, 20
Article 1, pp. 3, 13-15
Article 2, pp. 3, 17-21
Article 3, pp. 3, 23-29
Article 6, pp. 3, 24, 25, 31-37, 43
Articles of Confederation, p. 9
atheism, p. 33
atheists, pp. 35, 36
Australians, p. 51
authority (for bearing arms),
   pp. 47-48, 51
authorizing religion, pp. 43-45

B

Bacon, Leonard, p. 29
baptized humanism, p. 40

Barton, David, pp. 33, 42, 44
Bastiat, Fredrick, p. 50
Biblical court(s), pp. 26, 28-29
Biblical judges, pp. 28-29
biblically qualified men, p. 19
Biblical plan of salvation, p. 3*
Bill of Rights, pp. 39-42
body politic, p. 29
Bouvier's Law Dictionary, p. 49
British, p. 51
British kings, p. 10
Burger, Chief Justice Warren,
   pp. 25, 42
burglary, p. 49
Byles, Pastor Mather, p. 10
bystander, p. 50

C

cannibalism, p. 43
capital crimes, p. 33
capital felons, p. 55
capital punishment(s), pp. 29, 36,
   53-56
case law, p. 28
Charter of the United Nations,
   p. 33
Christendom, p. 37
Christendom (1st-century), p. 45
Christian Constitutionalists, pp. 7,
   23, 33, 61-62

---

*Subject found in footnote.

77

*Subject found in footnote.

*Subject found in footnote.

Scripture Index

*Scripture found in footnote.

*Scripture found in footnote.

---

*Scripture found in footnote.

ABOUT THE AUTHOR

Ted R. Weiland pastors Christian Covenant Fellowship in Scottsbluff, Nebraska, and is the evangelistic head of Mission to Israel Ministries. In addition to presiding over an international audio ministry, he lectures throughout the United States, has appeared on television and radio, and has authored twenty-two books.

For speaking engagements, he may be contacted at tweiland@vista beam.com.